"If you're facing a midlife job transition, *The Age Advantage* is the guide you've been searching for. In this informative and motivational book, Jean Walker will show you how to celebrate the advantages of a midlife career switch while she guides you through each stage of the transition—from the emotional shock that accompanies joblessness, to the fulfillment of securing your new dream career."

—Ken Dychtwald, Ph.D.,
founder, president, and CEO, Age Wave, LLC;
author of *Age Wave* and *Age Power: How the 21st Century Will Be Ruled by the New Old*

The Age Advantage

Making the Most of Your Midlife Career Transition

Jean Erickson Walker, Ed.D.

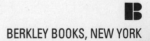

BERKLEY BOOKS, NEW YORK

The case studies presented in the book reflect real people and real situations;
however, the names of clients have been changed to protect their privacy.

This book is an original publication of The Berkley Publishing Group.

A Berkley Book / published by arrangement with the author

PRINTING HISTORY
Berkley trade paperback edition / September 2000

The Penguin Putnam Inc. World Wide Web site address is
http://www.penguinputnam.com

ISBN: 0-425-17645-2

BERKLEY®
Berkley Books are published by The Berkley Publishing Group,
a division of Penguin Putnam Inc.,
375 Hudson Street, New York, New York 10014.
BERKLEY and the "B" design
are trademarks belonging to Penguin Putnam Inc.

PRINTED IN THE UNITED STATES OF AMERICA

10 9 8 7 6 5 4 3 2 1

To my clients past, present and future.
May their tomorrows always be full of
hope and promise.

Acknowledgments

To my Pathways/OI Partners associates:

Kelly Pellegrini, whose faith is boundless and support never failing;

Merna Reynolds, who switched effortlessly from techie to photographer of the cover photo;

Jocelyn Dietz, whose calm poise keeps us all on track;

Lucy Z. Martin, cheerleader and role model for what a career entrepreneur can really mean;

David Sellers, psychologist and wise friend;

Ron Ennis, for the clients we shared and the hours we spent finding solutions to their professional struggles, and ours.

To my agent, Doris Michaels, whose energy and enthusiasm never waver and whose belief in the project was firm from the very beginning.

To my editor, Lisa Considine, who painstakingly shared her enormous gifts of professionalism and expertise and patiently insisted on clarity above all.

To my OI Partners worldwide who every day provide wise and caring counsel to people in career transition and who are always there for each other as friends and professional associates extraordinaire.

And always, and foremost, to my family, who makes everything worth doing and every tomorrow worth anticipating:

My husband, George, our children Cheryl, Erick, and Julie, Julie's husband, Chris, and their children, Cricket and Erick;

My parents and grandparents, who taught me always to keep learning and growing.

Contents

The Age
Advantage

The New Midlife Crisis

"This time, like all times, is a very good one,
if we but know what to do with it."
—RALPH WALDO EMERSON

WHEN we used to talk about midlife crisis, it meant dealing with the startling realization of mortality. It meant the line of pills beside your orange juice was lengthening. It meant your friends were looking older and you avoided the mirror as the day wore on and wrinkles deepened. It meant looking back nostalgically on sleeping through the night. And it meant saying good-bye to getting a second wind when you were climbing a mountain trail. It didn't mean worrying about having a job, however, and it certainly didn't mean starting a new career. It meant you were headed for the end, work-wise.

The last two decades changed all that. It is a rare American of mid age who has not either lost a job or been close to someone who has in the last few years. At least an equal number have left their jobs to seek new careers, start a business, or go out on their own as consultants, taking advantage of the professional opportunities and the personal flexibility offered by the virtual workplace. We are living longer, healthier lives and for many of us work we enjoy sounds far more interesting than retirement.

At the same time the pool of available jobs in the positions and salary ranges we find attractive is shrinking dramatically due to technology and the increasing shift of jobs from full-time employment to outsourcing. Another factor is new organizational structures that eliminate mid-level management positions, and mergers and acquisitions that cut duplicated positions.

The whole culture of the workplace is changing. During the economic doldrums of the eighties, companies began to rethink their relationship with employees. The implied contracts of the past that guaranteed lifetime employment, with a handshake, a gold watch, and a pension at the end, came to a screeching halt as they faced the undeniable fact that employees were their biggest expense item.

The whole economy underwent enormous changes, but by far the greatest impact was on the most financially and emotionally stable members of our society, those between the ages of forty and sixty, who lost job security, self-confidence, and a clear picture of the future. A midlife crisis changed from realizing you were not as young as you used to be to rolling up your sleeves and hitting the streets to look for a job.

The economy survived and eventually began to soar. New jobs were created, and by the late 1990s, the unemployment rate hit its lowest point in over twenty-five years. In the process, corporate America discovered a new strategy for increasing profits while decreasing expenses. It was the business management "aha!" of the century. Companies no longer need to guarantee lifelong employment to workers, or develop young employees. Why bother when they can hire them ready-made? Companies bring in people who can do a specific job right now, with little or no learning curve, and then turn them back out on the job market a few years or even a few months later when they no longer need them. There is very little overhead, no long-term commitment, minimal training, no pensions or health care or even medical insurance to worry about. Expenses can be predicted in strict relationship to potential income. Profits are clean and sure. Why didn't we think of this earlier? America has moved from an industrial society to a technological society and all the rules have changed. The era of a "Company of One" and multiple professional liaisons has begun, and as a result, contingent labor is predicted to make up 60 percent of our workforce early in the new century.

Although the culture of the workplace has changed, it's not all bad, because it means people are taking charge of their own lives, and for those who see the potential and the excitement this offers, it's a great time. The good news is the majority of people who go through a midlife career transition look back on it positively. It *is* a major life change, and the truth is most people try to avoid such changes. However, difficult as it may be, it's also a fresh start, an opportunity to begin again, to redefine who you really are, and who you want to be.

Over the last ten years I have worked with thousands of people in midlife career transition (some choose to leave their jobs, most have the choice made for them). They come to me with a wide range of backgrounds, from senior executives, managers, and business owners to consultants, salaried, and hourly workers. They come from companies that range in size from small entrepreneurships to Fortune 500 national and international corporations.

Regardless of their former positions, the size of the company, or their field of expertise, those who love life find the spark within themselves not only to meet the challenge, but to thrive on it. Others need a little help. Not all find jobs right away; not all find jobs that are the equivalent in pay or status. Some go through personal traumas including divorce, depression, and even losing their homes, but nearly without exception, they tell me they are happier afterward than they have ever been, because they have found out who they are, and they like what they have found. For the first time they are in charge of their lives, and it's a good feeling. Instead of looking forward to the end of work, they are looking forward to each day. When they quit focusing on a specific date for retirement, they also discover their options expand. They don't *have* to earn the same salary or work the same hours. Pat M., age fifty-five, recently accepted a position in Beijing, China, where he is directing the building and operation of five power plants. When I asked him how long he intended to stay in China, he replied, "Forever . . . or as long as I'm having fun." Retirement holds no appeal for Pat; life is just too interesting.

Who Is the Midlife Career Transitioner?

Midlife is a moving target, including the "youngsters" who are surprised to find age discrimination waiting on the other side of forty, the "elders" in their late fifties and early sixties, and, of course, the "Baby Boomers" who are hitting fifty and midlife like a tidal wave. Midlife is obviously in the eye of the beholder. Let me tell you about some of my clients.

John S., forty-two, is a timber worker who lives in a small mill town in Oregon. He recently lost his job; so have his father and most of his friends. Environmental concerns for old-growth forest, spawning beds for salmon, and even the spotted owl have led to serious downsizing and the mill has closed. The mill really *is* the town; without the jobs it provides, the employment outlook is grim. John has never looked for a job in his life. He started work at the mill at sixteen when his father got him a job on the line, and he has learned the business from the ground up. He has no illusions about the employment potential in a mill town where everyone else is out of work. For John, career transition means moving to where the jobs are, perhaps even overseas, where his skills are in high demand.

Carol M. is thirty-nine. She was a mid-level marketing manager in a high-tech firm, the first woman ever promoted to that position in her company. Ambitious, energetic, and hard-driving, she has worked hard to prove herself and has earned the respect of both her employees and her supervisors. However, the company has just been acquired, and as is common in such cases, the managers in the smaller company are out of jobs. Carol has very little hope of replacing her salary or her title . . . at least at this point. So she is going back to school to complete her MBA in order to add academic credentials to her impressive work experience.

Ken W. is fifty-six. He was with a telecommunications company for twenty-seven years. He climbed the corporate ladder and took early retirement four years ago. Ken was still looking for a job when he came to see me, but he'd about given up. It seems everything about his experience was working against him. He was with the same company and away from the technical part of the business far too long. He also fits the category of mid-level management that is being eliminated. There really aren't a lot of traditional jobs out there for him. For Ken, the answer was to reposition himself. Realizing he had managed projects throughout his career, I recommended that he join the Project Management Institute and seek certification as a project management professional. Six months later, after long hours burning the midnight oil, he took his exam, passed with flying

colors, and renewed his job search. The results were
impressive. He signed on for a three-month contract
position, which turned into a full-time position. Two
years later he is making nearly 50 percent more than he
was in his last position, and having a lot more fun.

Barbara B. is sixty-four. Barbara's husband died a
couple of months ago, just as he was getting ready to
retire. Her husband had a company pension. She doesn't.
Her husband had company medical benefits. She doesn't.
Barbara was the perfect corporate wife, following her
husband to fourteen cities as he climbed the corporate
ladder. She was his major support system, establishing the
home, enrolling the children in new schools, finding new
doctors, doing volunteer work, the kind of person our
communities and families depend upon. Now she has to
fend for herself. She has a fine-arts degree that is forty-
two years old, but she has never worked outside the
home. She knows that she will have to support herself for
twenty to thirty years, but how? The answer for Barbara
is working for a local nonprofit organization, where her
contacts and record as a volunteer have led to a job as
"coordinator of volunteers."

Bill A., a manufacturing manager for over thirty
years, is fifty-six. Bill is one of those people others refer
to as the salt of the earth. He is a strong, competent
person who is liked and respected by everyone he meets.
His company is eliminating one of its manufacturing
lines. There are two managers; Bill has been there the
longest and makes the most money, so he's the one who
loses his job. Perhaps the most humiliating thing for Bill
was being escorted out of the building past his crews.
For a while he suffered from serious depression, but his
energy is back now, and with it the determination to get
a job doing what he loves. He has recently accepted a

position to move a manufacturing plant from one state to another. It's only a six-month project, but he knows he'll enjoy the work and it'll look great on his résumé.

Robert S. is fifty-four. He is the former president of a $20 million construction company. When profits took a downturn, the board of directors decided to replace him. Yes, he got a golden parachute . . . nearly platinum, in fact. However, he would much rather have a job, with the perks, the prestige, the challenges, and the ego gratification that go with it. He certainly isn't interested in retirement, but there aren't many positions at his level, so he's considering consulting as a way of keeping current until the right full-time position comes along.

My oldest client is seventy-four. *Frank R.* retired as a bank vice-president a few years ago. He is a very busy man. He plays a lot of golf but he also manages to put in a minimum of twenty hours a week in volunteer service. He takes two to three trips a year with Elder Hostel. He even bought a new organ with a computer program and he spends time each day writing music. But he's bored. Frank misses the world of business. Recently, he came up with an idea for a radar gadget that will fit on the front of golf carts to show obstacles on the golf course. Now he's talking to engineers and plans to start his own company soon.

These people are all in midlife career transition. They are all people for whom age is a factor in their job search and in their consideration of other options. Whether age is an advantage or a disadvantage has as much to do with their attitudes as it does with the reality. Perhaps that is because our attitudes become our realities. When is midlife? It varies from person to person. Somewhere around the mid-century mark seems to be the most common definition, but as we see with the stories above, it may range as low as the late thirties and as high as the early seventies.

Whenever we reach midlife can be a wonderful time, for it provides the opportunity to gain perspective on who and what we are, regardless of how others may see us. A career transition should be just that, a "transition," not a crisis. It is a time of knowing, of evaluating how we've met past challenges, recognizing that the current one is equally manageable, and then beginning a new and better life. The uncertainty of youth is gone, and in its place is something we call wisdom. We accept ourselves. We even learn to chuckle fondly *with* ourselves rather than laugh *at* ourselves with self-ridicule that masks the insecurities of youth.

Enjoy yourself. These are the "good old days" you're going to miss a few years down the road.

How Do You Find a Job at Midlife?

General strategies and techniques designed for finding a job simply do not work for someone who is mid-age. You are probably not a novice in your field, and the overeager, overenthusiastic approach advocated for younger workers is simply inappropriate. You may well be interviewed by someone much younger and less experienced than you are, and your challenge is to come across with dignity, without appearing too authoritative and risking intimidating the interviewer. It's a delicate balancing act.

Change is never easy, and for those of us I call the "ity" generation, it's even more difficult. We grew up in a culture that valued the virtues of dependabil*ity*, reliabil*ity*, stabil*ity*, predictabil*ity*, and secur*ity*. We were taught to stand on our own two feet, so it's difficult for us to ask for help. That doesn't mesh well with the fact that 80 percent of jobs are acquired through networking!

Many of us have been in the same field, or even the same company, for the majority of our careers, and it's hard to imagine doing anything else or even realizing we have options. With mortgages, kids in college, elderly parents to care for, and friends who expect us to continue on the same social track, it's easy to fall into the trap of thinking that the next step is to find a job . . . any job . . . that will pay the bills. But you're much too special to settle for that. Midlife is a wonderful time for introspection, for gathering new knowledge of this incredible being you've lived with so long, and for finally putting all your talents, interests, and abilities together for the most productive and fulfilling years of your life. This is a book about understanding yourself, the role work plays in your life, and the marketplace where your talents and skills will be most appreciated. It's about positioning yourself for the future you want.

Midlife may not be the right age to retire or to climb a corporate ladder; but it is just the right age to take control of your life. This book is for people who look forward to making the third third of their lives the best time of all. It is for people, like you and me, who care about the quality of our lives. It is for those of us who are at mid-age, at the top of the hill, where the view is best. Indeed, as the Greek philosopher Syrus said so long ago, "It takes a long time to bring excellence to maturity."

CHAPTER ONE

Dealing with Change and Transition

"All the significant battles are waged with in the self."

—SHELDON KOPP

THE alarm goes off, you climb out of bed and prepare for another day at work, not much different than any other day. Except that today is your last day. By three o'clock, you'll be on your way home, desk cleared, computer access denied, credit card in pieces. You'll walk past your coworkers, and see your own pain reflected in their eyes. Some will suddenly be very busy. Others will get emotional, stumbling in their attempts to comfort you and themselves. The grapevine is alive and well, and something kept very secret until an hour ago is now common knowledge.

Your manager called you into his office, and when you got there the human-resource manager was with him.

"John, I'm sorry, but your position has been eliminated. The company is going through a reorganization, and we are letting people go who are no longer essential to our operation. We appreciate the work you've done for Allied all these years, and we'll be providing you with a severance package to carry you through until you find another job. Mary will explain your benefits to you and give you your final check. Good luck. I know you won't have any trouble finding work."

Not have any trouble finding work? You think, "But *this* is where I work. It's where I've worked my whole adult life. I've never actually looked for a job. I wouldn't know what to do anyplace else, and I certainly don't want to begin again at my age." As you turn into your driveway, you wonder how you will explain it all to your wife when it makes no sense to you.

Regardless of whether or not leaving a job was your decision, the result is the same. Your regular paycheck is gone and dealing with the reality may be much more difficult than you ever imagined. Few who are *fired,* or *downsized,* or *restructured,* or *merged* out of a job had any idea the ax was about to fall, and that makes it all the harder. In most instances, they had no reason to believe they were not "essential" to the operation. They dwell on this point over and over in discussions with their families, friends, and career counselors. They talk about the projects they were working on, the idiosyncrasies of equipment or procedures no one else knows, and they take a certain amount of comfort in believing the company doesn't fully comprehend what it's doing. Their old boss will certainly come to his senses and ask them back. The truth . . . hard as it is to accept . . . is that companies are like lakes. When you draw a bucket of water from a lake, it adjusts very quickly, and when someone leaves a company, it isn't long before it adapts. In my work with people in career transition, I've seen only a handful of clients asked to return (and in a number of these cases, my clients had been so successful exploring other options that they had much more attractive offers—surely the most satisfying revenge of all!).

A job loss brings shock, dismay, disbelief, and certainly denial. The anger and the bitterness come later. Somewhere in between, self-doubt raises its ugly head. These emotions are all part of the healing process, but occasionally, they begin to take on a life of their own, growing until they smother everything in their way. Accepting reality is critical to successful transitions.

Change is difficult under any circumstances, but because work is such an integral part of who we are and how we see ourselves, dealing with an unexpected job loss can be devastating. Nevertheless, we're all going to have to get used to the process, because it isn't just the poor performers who are being fired; it's you and I, and our friends and neighbors. Job security isn't based on long-term relationships; it's based on the corporate mantra: "What can you do for me today and tomorrow?" That means everyone needs to be ready for change because it is a permanent state of affairs. Not only success, but survival, will depend upon taking control of your career, and keeping yourself marketable.

Clients often tell me, "I want to find a stable company, where I can work until I retire." I hate to break the news, but that's a naive expectation. Careers, not jobs, are what we need to think about. No longer can anyone expect a company to assume responsibility for making our career decisions, moving us like chess pieces on a board. The good news is that by putting yourself in charge, you'll build a career that reflects your own interests and talents rather than attempting to mold them to an employer's needs.

Dispelling the Traditional View of Life

Today's work world provides enormous opportunities to rethink how we want to structure the phases of our lives. Traditionally, we have divided life very neatly into three stages: Preparation for Life, Adult Life, and End of Life (retirement), each of them approximately twenty-five years long. During Preparation for Life, our focus was on education, socialization, and training for the future. It was all about learning and growth, about exploration and discovery. Play was not only recreation, but an opportunity to develop skills.

Adult Life focused on duty, responsibility, work, family, contributing to the general welfare of society. Security and stability were highly valued; risk was something to be avoided at all costs. Theoretically, education was unnecessary, and play was inappropriate.

Retirement was a gradual easing out at the End of Life, a time touted as "freedom to do what you've always wanted to do." Never mind that most people had absolutely no idea what that was; they'd been too busy doing their jobs to have time to develop other interests. Rest, leisure, play, and even education designed as play were considered appropriate for people who were no longer active participants in "real" life.

The concept of a basic right to retirement has kept innumerable people in jobs they hate. The myth said retirees would have enough money to travel, enough time to play golf or work in the garden all day—in short, the End of Life would be a time of sunshine and roses. It said nothing of repetitious days, boredom, and growing apathy. The problem with tradition is that we don't question its validity often enough. We're conditioned to believe certain things, we inherit expectations and fulfill them without questioning whether or not they make any sense.

Life lived to its fullest isn't confined to stages. Rather, it is continuing cycles of learning and discovery, meaningful work, play, and relaxation. The traditional view of life no longer fits our lifestyles. We're not willing to prescribe activities for particular stages. We're much more interested in finding a balance between work, relaxation, and learning, the highest priority of job seekers today, regardless of age.

Midlifers start second and third careers because their work is such an integral part of their lives. They seek opportunities to fulfill their "life's work," to welcome challenges and look forward to the future rather than disengage from active involvement. It's true that the new workplace is less than stable and that you can't count on the company that writes your paycheck for security. It's entirely possible, however, that we'll all be happier, more productive, more energized people when we find stability and security within ourselves as we build stronger, more reliable foundations for our lives. The first step is to accept change and learn to deal effectively with the ambiguity of transition.

Understanding Change: Life's Only Certainty

Change is abrupt; transition is prolonged. Too often, people get stuck at the change, and forget to move through the transition. When that happens, they are immobilized, a little like a trapeze artist who decides to stop in the middle of a swing; a dangerous place to be, particularly if there's no safety net below! You lose momentum, you lose confidence, you lose direction, and there you hang, with nowhere to go but down.

Think of transitions as bridges that take you from firm footing on one side to the other. First of all, you have to believe there really will be something on the other side. That means checking it out beforehand. Next, you have to prepare for the trip. That includes knowing yourself, because you're the one leading it. Third, you'd better recognize it when you get there.

Transitions don't happen in a day. They take place over a prolonged period of time and may last much longer than you anticipated. Clients often tell me, "I'd be enjoying this, if I just knew when it would be over." I wish I knew, but transitions are like the fog. They come and they go; sometimes there's a break, and you're sure it's going to clear up, and then it socks back in and you can't see a thing. Like traffic on a two-lane bridge, once you make the commitment to start across, you just have to accept the speed of the flow. You can't pass, you don't dare slow down, and you certainly can't jump off!

One thing you can do, however, is to understand the phenomena of transitions, and examine your own nature, so you can maneuver across the bridge without panicking. Transitions divide naturally into three phases: beginnings, middles, and endings. Most people are more comfortable, energized, and productive in one of them than the others, whether it is a career transition, a project, or even a relationship. Understanding this natural bias not only helps with the career transition, but helps you make the right career choice.

Beginnings People thrive on planning and organizing. They are creative, with big imaginations and high energy. They're the visionaries of the world. They love starting projects, but often have difficulty finishing them. Because they crave stimulation, they are easily bored in maintenance-type jobs. With their high energy and multitude of ideas, other people think of them as leaders. When they are in transition, however, they can be more like spinning tops, whirling out of control, bouncing from one idea to the next.

Beginnings People love career transitions. The danger is that they tend to make decisions much too quickly, without really thinking through the consequences. They need to be reminded to focus on their ultimate goal.

Middles People thrive on stability, security, and routine

and are uncomfortable outside them. They base their decisions on the known and fear change above all things. The backbone of organizations, they're both predictable and dependable. They rarely initiate anything and hate to see anything come to an end. They are at their best in the "middle," surrounded by the past and the future, snug in their nests. When they face a transition, they dread entering it and equally dread leaving it, because both places call for decisions, something they would much rather leave to others.

Career transitions are particularly difficult for Middles People, as they are pushed out of their nests and left without guidance and direction. They can easily become victims of what I call "Transition Syndrome": vague feelings of malaise, headaches, digestive problems, low energy, and even depression. They may even find it difficult to leave the house or to talk to people; they just want to crawl into their caves and stay there. One senior manager in his late forties didn't leave the house for three weeks after he lost his job. He told me that coming to my office was the hardest thing he'd ever done, but he had awakened that morning with the realization that he either had to come and see me or go to the hospital. He was scared and couldn't handle it alone anymore. When Middles People do eventually embark on a new beginning, it's a long time before they feel comfortable.

Endings People like bringing closure. They are great implementers, moving straight through the project, never losing track of the goal. Endings People relish awards, certificates, and ceremonies, because they represent a successful completion, another notch on their belts.

A transition for them is something to be gotten over, so they "can get on with it." The danger is that they can miss the big picture because they're so focused on the immediate goal, racing through life, adding up check marks, and rarely stopping to smell the roses. In career transition, this may create serious problems as they have a tendency to accept the first job offer, whether or not it's the right one. On the plus side, they're generally pretty easily satisfied, far less particular than either Beginnings or Middles People. The only thing they really can't stand is to be micromanaged, or to work in a bureaucracy that keeps them from getting things done.

The career transition brings out basic tendencies—tendencies you can use to target particular jobs and industries. Beginnings People are happiest in entrepreneurial companies, particularly those that pride themselves on being on the "cutting edge" of new development. Their conceptual abilities are invaluable and their "out of the box" thinking creates opportunities. They should avoid traditional, rule-bound organizations where other staff members are quick to point out "how we do things around here."

Middles People are happiest in cultures with definite rules, policies, and procedures, such as government work, education, banks, health care, or utilities. Unfortunately, these are currently the most difficult jobs to find. Most available positions are in small companies, where everyone is expected to do multiple tasks, the most difficult environment for Middles People. The advantage of small companies, however, is the relatively short time it takes to feel at home. I always advise Middles People to consider a small company, but to be sure the job is very clearly defined.

Endings People make great project managers and often prefer contract work. They don't have a lot of patience with people who are just learning. They would much rather work with professionals who produce quickly and efficiently. Typically, Endings People are focused on the immediate task, not on the big picture or the people involved. This is not to say they can't be effective team players, but getting the job done and moving on to the next is their forte.

Knowing yourself and whether you are a Beginnings, Middles, or Endings person can help you deal with your own idiosyncrasies. An advantage of age is recognizing where we excel, and not being intimidated by our own weaknesses. In other words, we have learned not to take ourselves too seriously.

Change Creates a Confused Reality

We are all creatures of habit. We like what we're used to. We may be in a rut but, whether or not it's comfortable, it's ours. Change makes us uncomfortable. It's scary. Transition can make us feel disoriented, but understanding the nature of the beast can make it easier to deal with it.

Work largely determines the patterns of our lives. Some people live to work; others work to live; still others think their work *is* their life. Regardless of what role work plays in your life, there's no question that it dominates your life. Days are filled by tasks created by other people; identities are wrapped up in the company and the people around us. When a job ends, the framework of our lives disappears, and we are left isolated and alone. Everything falls apart.

It's easy to expect the worst. When one thing goes wrong (such as losing a job), it's easy to focus selectively on the clouds and not see the sun peeking through. Change brings the unknown hurtling like a meteor into our lives. It is often abrupt, frequently unexpected, usually disconcerting. It's not, however, the *End,* so take a deep breath, keep an open mind, and try not to expect the worst. You can't ignore, harness, or escape it. You have to deal with it.

Develop the attitude that things will probably turn out well. It takes more muscles to cry than to laugh, and at midlife, who needs more wrinkles? Try to look at the big picture. Hey, maybe this is the opportunity you've been waiting for!

Your family and friends are part of your career transition.

The unknown can be frightening for them, too. Don't forget to bring them into the process. Parents too often try to protect their children (keep them in the dark?) from painful situations. In doing so, they're also preventing them from sharing the opportunity for learning and growth. Some experts predict people just entering the workforce will have as many as eight to ten different jobs during their work life. For them, transitions will be more like milestones than crises. There's no question parents are role models for their children; if they don't share their thoughts and feelings with them during this career transition process, they deny them the opportunity to prepare for their own future.

Even the youngest children know when their parents are upset. They want to be included, and they want to help.

Jane W. is a single parent whose sons were nine and eleven when she lost her job at the Trojan Nuclear Plant. Her oldest son had always been a marginal C student, so she thought there was some mistake when he brought home straight A's the term after her job ended. He told her he wanted to make her feel better.

Howard F. worked as a facilities supervisor at a major grocery-store chain. The company decided to outsource his work and he was laid off after sixteen years with the company. The next night he came home to find his car washed, and dinner on the table. His teenage son just wanted Dad to feel better.

Withholding news of your job loss from your family rarely does more than isolate them.

Steve R. didn't tell his six- and eight-year-old children about losing his job for over two weeks. He didn't know how to tell them he'd been fired and he couldn't bear the thought that they'd be disappointed in him. He hoped he'd be able to find a job quickly and they'd never have to know. It wasn't long before they learned the truth from neighbor children, however, but were afraid to ask him about it. I finally convinced him to talk to them, and far from being disappointed in him, the family drew closer as they faced the transition together.

Spouses can have the most difficult time of all. Their lives are thrown into turmoil and their reactions can vary from calm acceptance to solicitous support, from exaggerated cheerfulness and optimism to resentment and bitterness.

Larry B. is a tall, handsome, confident sales manager. When Larry lost his job, it brought back frightening memories for his wife, Linda. Her father had lost his job thirty years before, when she was a sophomore in high school. The family had been forced to sell their home and move into a tiny apartment, a traumatic experience she never forgot. She was convinced history was repeating itself. Together, Larry and I involved her in the career counseling process and gradually her fear turned to confidence. In fact, she eventually became interested in reviving her own professional career.

Mike L. is a thirty-nine-year-old bundle of nervous energy. He was fired from three jobs in less than four years, largely because of his tendency to tell it like it is, whether or not anyone wants to hear his opinion. He was convinced his predicament was everyone else's fault, until the last dismissal, when he really fell apart. Afraid to go home to his wife and two children, he went to his parents' house. Moments after he walked through the door, he burst into tears. This strong, sometimes arrogant man fell to the floor hyperventilating. His parents rushed him to the emergency room and called his wife. They were surprised to hear her say, "I'm tired of dealing with it." Mike and his wife had a long struggle ahead of them. He spent several months working on his communication skills before I felt he was ready to go on with his job search. In the meantime, he and his wife worked to improve their own communication. When she began to see a change in his outlook, her own faith in their future improved. Mike is doing well in his new job with a company that values his expertise.

Joan M. is a highly accomplished, very professional finance executive who recently married a successful banker. At age forty-two, she moved to a new city and started a new life, fully expecting to find a job comparable to her previous one. Unfortunately, openings were few, and she couldn't seem to make it past the first interview. Her husband, Fred, stepped in to take charge of the project, much to her distress, and nearly ended their new marriage. He got up early each morning, picked up the paper, and selected the openings he wanted her to apply for each day. He'd cut them out, tape them to a piece of paper, and make notes about how she was to approach each one. When he returned from work, he'd quiz her on the day's calls. Obviously, this was not the best way to win friends (or keep a wife!). In Joan's case, I spent as much time counseling Fred on how to be supportive without taking control as I did helping her find a new job.

Larry E. was determined to find a job immediately when his position as head counsel of a utility company was eliminated. His wife, Sue, however, encouraged him to take some time off and really think about his career. She had questioned for some time whether he really enjoyed his work, but he had been reluctant to take a chance on starting his own law practice. With her full support (she went back to work for a couple of years while he got his start), he was able to follow his dreams.

People can be supportive and encouraging and even offer constructive ideas, but the reality is that only you can manage your own career transition. The best thing loved ones can do is to have faith in your ability to do so.

You can make the career transition easier for everyone by limiting the amount of time you spend talking about your old job or employer. If you were unexpectedly let go, this transition can assume monumental proportions, becoming all-encompassing. Keep discussions of the past and plans for the future to normal working hours, using evenings and weekends to connect with the rest of the world.

In order for there to be a new beginning, there must be an ending. It is important to bring closure to the past. Looking back over the highs and lows of your old job will probably bring both laughter and tears, but regardless of the emotions that surface, take time to make your peace with the past. Dump the baggage and prepare for a fresh start.

Personal and professional growth begin by understanding the dynamics of change and transition. Don't be afraid of the future; create it!

Up, Up, and Away!

Imagine a hot air balloon, tethered but ready to soar. You are in the basket, looking up. There is an expectancy, an urgency, an excitement as you imagine yourself floating far above the treetops, at one with the eagles in their clifftop aeries. Where will you go?

Now imagine the ropes anchoring your balloon to the

ground. What is holding you down? What keeps you from reaching your dreams? Label each of the ropes after an anchor in your own life. Which are essential to your happiness and well-being? Which give you stability and grounding?

Make your choices. Cut the ropes you no longer want or need. Dare to risk a new kind of life because you believe in yourself and trust in the future.

It's time to move forward, to build new relationships, to establish new routines, to learn new skills, and to stretch your limits. Midlife career transition is the opportunity to throw wide the door to ideas and feelings, and to discover careers you never imagined possible. The future is full of challenges just waiting for you . . . but first you must believe in yourself.

CHAPTER TWO

Career Options and Lifestyle Choices

*"There are no secrets to success. It is the
result of preparation, hard work, learning
from failure."*
—GENERAL COLIN L. POWELL

THE biggest obstacle to successful midlife career transition is believing you have no options. The reality is you have the experience and proven track record for a wide range of possibilities, but although you have confidence in your ability to meet enormous challenges in most areas of your life, the very idea of looking for a job may give you cold chills.

The first reaction for most people when they lose a job is panic, immediately followed by determination to find another as quickly as possible. They want to fix what is broken, preferably before friends and associates find out what's happened. A long job search can be particularly difficult for someone who is mid-age. Their whole sense of self-respect is caught up in the job loss and they feel unwanted, rejected, and even more devastated personally than they are professionally. They begin to question their own competence, plagued by sneaky little thoughts: "Was I ever any good?" "Has my whole career been one big snow job?" " Will anyone ever hire me?"

Because of decades of work experience, people of mid-age often anticipate numerous offers . . . and quickly. They expect headhunters to call and old professional colleagues to line up to hire them. The phone, however, is unnaturally quiet. The bottom line is they are out of a job, it doesn't feel good, and they may be tempted to grab the first job that comes along. However, if the new job is not the right one, they'll be out on the street again before they find their way to the executive washroom. They'll be plunged into the emotional turmoil of the first job loss all over again, only this time it will be magnified, because they'll be convinced that: (1) they are losers, (2) the unluckiest people around, (3) the world's no good, or (4) their companies don't know what they're doing. Any one or all may be true, but thinking so isn't going to get them a job or make them feel any better.

"Exploring new opportunities" is the common fallback term. Actually, it's what everyone in midlife should be doing, regardless of whether they have lost a job, have a job they enjoy, or are contemplating leaving a job. Midlife is a major milestone in life, a place to consciously stop and reassess life values and goals. There is no question that a career path largely determines our role and place in society, and if it is the wrong one, it can feel like a cage with no escape. A major challenge of midlife is to find the *self* inside the image we have become to the outside world.

Midlife career transitions deserve total focus. Put off decisions until you are ready, emotionally as well as intellectually, to make them. Everyone has options. To assume your path is established at midlife and there is no deviating from it is to sell yourself short. Life is an ongoing evolution; don't let it "just happen." A job loss is traumatic, but it's not the end of the world. It may even be the beginning of a whole new, perhaps even better, life.

The advantage of midlife is that it offers a clear view of the past, and an informed perspective of the future. After all, you've had a lifetime of learning and growing, of successes and failures, of challenges and smooth passages. Decision making at its best requires self-confidence, and a large part of that confidence comes from our work. Being tossed out of a job at midlife is devastating, so you must restore your self-concept before you make serious decisions about your future.

People approach midlife with different attitudes. Some do it on autopilot. They believe their course is set, the instruments have taken over, and they're headed for a landing. An unexpected job loss throws them completely off course. If they've been employed in the same company for ten to twenty years, they've probably had very little choice in their career moves. They have simply, and faithfully, responded to the company's needs, and the wrench they feel at separation is apt to include strong feelings of betrayal. Pulling out of this quandary and taking charge of their careers may be the greatest challenge of their lives.

Others are just hanging on at midlife. One client described it as "a roller coaster at full speed." Nothing had turned out as he planned. His work life had been in turmoil for the past ten years as his company went from one management structure to another or, as he referred to them, "the flavors of the month." After twenty-four years, he and his wife had divorced. His last two or three relationships "just didn't work out." He'd exchanged a life that included a beautiful home with a view of the river and golf every weekend for a high-rise condo and an occasional workout. He no longer saw his old friends, and when he learned that his job was over, he realized his work associations were gone, too. Neither cruising on autopilot nor passively accepting life's blows is the ideal way to face midlife. It's time to take charge, to make conscious choices.

If one word could describe people at midlife, it would surely be "responsible." It is difficult for us to think of ourselves first, to let our own wants and needs take priority over everyone else's because it goes against our cultural upbringing. Adult life, with work, family, and community obligations, leaves us with little time for ourselves. Now, at midlife, it is easy to feel guilty about making choices based on what *we* want. Yet, the *greatest* responsibility we have in life is to reach our potential. To do that, we must value ourselves and listen to our own intuition, for if we just listen, the answers are within us. No one knows you like you know yourself. The problem for most of us at mid-age is that we have lost contact with ourselves. We need to remember that there is only one person who travels all of life's journey with us and that is the person whose judgment is most important. As people move in and out of our lives, they add depth and breadth to it. However, we are ultimately the masters of our fates. A midlife career transition is the time to pause, take stock, and then redefine our futures.

At midlife, we can look forward to twenty or thirty years of active involvement, wherever our interests lead us. Make your decision to evaluate the options, without preconceived opinions. That is the first step.

Defining the Options

People work for many reasons, but perhaps the only one that really counts is that we must, for without our work we are incomplete. Over the last few years I've seen a remarkable change in the way my clients answer the question "Why do you work?" Several years ago almost everyone answered that they worked to earn money to pay for expenses. That was their top priority. In these last five years, however, fewer and fewer clients mention salary or benefits in either workshops or individual counseling. Instead, they're saying:

"I like being productive."

"I enjoy what I do. I'd miss it if I couldn't work."

"I like being respected for my expertise. Only the people at my work really understand what it takes to be good at what I do."

We are becoming much more conscious of the intrinsic value of work, its relationship to our self-image, to our sense of belonging, and to our instinctive need to do something we consider worthwhile. Although the majority of us still expect to retire eventually, the closer we come to retirement eligibility, the less appealing the idea of leaving work becomes and we begin to explore options that include combinations of work, leisure activities, travel, and education. Know that it is unrealistic to make firm plans for the next thirty years; three-to-five-year plans make much more sense. As doors close, others open.

Let's say you're fifty-two and your last day of work was last week. Now is not an appropriate time to make major lifestyle changes. There must also be a time of healing. The feelings of betrayal and hurt, of anger and remorse, of panic and fear must be acknowledged, validated, and put into perspective. These emotions are normal; everyone has them to varying degrees, regardless of their financial situation or place in life. Respecting our feelings is a sign of strength, not weakness. With healing comes renewed energy; with renewed energy come powers of creative problem solving. Then cautious optimism begins to emerge and solutions begin to surface.

Will you look for a new job? Think about owning your own business or becoming a consultant? Are you ready for retirement? Let's look at the options.

Finding a Job

For some people, full-time employment may be the only logical choice. The quickest career transition, of course, is to find a job that is as close as possible to your last, but don't ignore the opportunity to explore other areas.

Finding the right job begins with developing three profiles: a Personal Profile, a Job Profile, and a Company Profile. I encourage clients to complete them in great detail, because the more information you include, the better the road map you'll create for your job search. These profiles all focus on knowing yourself and identifying situations when you were the most successful. At midlife, other people assume we know who we are and that we have a clear picture of our own interests, skills, and talents. However, I find the majority of my clients have given very little time or attention to determining exactly what suits them best. They've just done the job. For most, serious self-assessment is a new experience.

The Personal Profile is all about you, without regard to a specific job or industry. It begins with a long list of questions about your values, lifestyle preferences, and goals for the future, but it also includes questions about what you really enjoy doing, when you are the most energized and productive, when you feel the best and most look forward to going to work. In chapter 4, on Career Interests, there are several exercises that can help you develop this profile.

The next step is to create a profile of your ideal job, unrelated to a specific job title. Visualize yourself going about your duties; describe responsibilities, but also think about the company culture, environment, relationships with coworkers, travel and growth opportunities, status and compensation. Are you dealing with the public or working quietly in a back office? Be as specific as you can. Ultimately, you will use it to identify potential positions and compare offers.

The third step is to describe your ideal employer. The Company Profile should include information about the dominant management style, whether the culture is more corporate or entrepreneurial, conservative or flexible. How are decisions made? Does the product or service it offers match your own standards and values? Is it an innovative company, on the "cutting edge" of futuristic thinking, or does it pride itself on tradition? Is the industry in a growth mode? Will you be bringing expertise to a young company, or will you be gaining new experience there? The ideal situation for many midlife career transitioners is to work for a company where they have solid background in the field, but will also be learning new technology or techniques.

These three profiles, Personal Profile, Job Profile, and Company Profile, are the foundation of your job search. The job market for the future is looking increasingly optimistic, with some industries complaining about a *lack* of qualified workers. In today's job market, the person at midlife can have a distinct advantage. Experience gives them a short learning curve, a real plus to companies on the move.

Working full-time is not the only option. Contingent employment is the fastest-growing field in the United States. It describes any part-time or contract employee who is employed for a specific time frame and ranges from CEOs brought in to turn around a company to entry-level data processing jobs, and nearly everything in between. As far back as March 3, 1993, *USA Today* quoted Richard Belous, vice-president and chief economist at the National Planning Association, predicting temporary workers would be 35 percent of the workforce by the year 2000. Since then, futurists have crept toward higher figures, ranging from 40 to 60 percent of the workforce by 2020.

Contract and contingency work may mesh well with your plans to travel, continue your education, take time off, or even alternate among these. Plus, you don't need to work as hard to provide financial security for your retirement years if you are able to extend the length of your employment years. You also gain the added benefit of keeping current in your field and retaining your professional status and interests.

Too often, job seekers at midlife are willing to take any position just to end the search. This is not only unnecessary; it's a waste of talent. I frequently hear clients say, "I just have a few years left until I'm sixty-two, so it really doesn't matter what I do until then." Why would anyone want to waste years in an unrewarding job? At midlife you have the time, the energy, and the talent to select the *right* job.

Owning a Business

The All-American Dream is owning your own business; whether it turns out to be a dream or a nightmare depends largely upon you, but you should know the success rate for start-up businesses is less than encouraging. Over 85 percent fail in the first five years, the majority within the first two years. Chances for success are best for people with experience in the field and even better for those with enough financial backing to support the business (and themselves) for a minimum of three years. No start-up operator should expect to make a profit the first year as any funds over and above expenses will probably need to go right back into the business.

Your potential for success is greatly heightened if you are:

- Independent, self-directed, self-motivated, and self-disciplined

- Highly organized, able to set priorities and establish and meet deadlines consistently.

- Credible, well respected, and trusted

- A good communicator

- An experienced business manager

- A skilled marketer

- Recognized for expertise in your field

- An active and successful networker

- Self assured and confident

- Energetic, productive, and able to work effectively without a support system

- Financially stable

People become business owners by buying an established business, purchasing a franchise, or starting a new business (the purest form of "entrepreneurship" and also the most risky).

Buying a business requires solid professional help. Bringing in experts for due diligence, legal and financial advice, and projections on the market is absolutely critical. Be aware that more and more companies are making business decisions with the express purpose of luring prospective buyers. A business that looks profitable at a glance may be just steps ahead of its creditors. If the company is unwilling to allow you to bring in your own analysis team, you should start to wonder if there are things they would prefer that you not discover.

Purchasing an established franchise is the most secure form of business ownership because it comes with a proven track record, an established market identity, and ongoing support. Like buying a business, however, it pays to work through a franchise broker who can guide you in matching your own interests and skills with the right franchise. Select a broker who is licensed and be sure to interview his or her former clients to see how satisfied they are with the support they received.

Entrepreneurship is the most creative of the business ownership options. It's starting from scratch, so the time from start-up to profitability ranges from almost immediately to possibly never. There are no guarantees. The upside is that it's all yours. You make all the decisions and the profits are yours alone. The downside is also that it's all yours. The risk is great. People who choose this option generally have a distinct distaste for taking orders from anyone and are confident they really do have a better mousetrap. Whether the world will beat a path to their door is the question. Having the financial wherewithal to put a business together (and to survive if it doesn't take off!) is critical. It certainly helps when there's a second income in the family and when your loved ones wholeheartedly support the undertaking.

Owning your own business is a roller-coaster ride. The highs are higher than anywhere else; the lows are lower. It's exciting, challenging, frustrating, exhausting, never-ending . . . and exactly right for some people. Later in the book I'll discuss ways you can determine your own Entrepreneurial Quotient and then lay out strategies for making your own business work.

Becoming a Consultant

Consulting is a natural for people in midlife career transition who have a level of knowledge and skill that is recognized and respected by other people in the field. There's also a certain appeal to presenting yourself to the world as an "expert!" Proclaiming yourself a consultant can also be a euphemism for being unemployed and having trouble finding a job. Whether or not that is the case, hiring managers and recruiters, perhaps even your friends, may make that assumption. Hanging out your shingle is not enough. You must be serious about becoming a consultant if you are going to have any credibility, and that means identifying a market niche and committing at least three to five years to building a clientele. You'll need a professional marketing campaign, support staff, and an office. With these things in place, consulting can be fascinating, challenging, full of variety . . . and yes, even profitable.

A downside to consulting is that it can also be very lonely. This is the most common complaint I hear from people who have spent most of their professional lives in the corporate world. Unless you join a group of consultants, you are likely to be spending most of your time alone. Marketing your services will take up to 50 percent of your time. Another 25 percent will be spent managing the business, writing proposals, advertising, and bookkeeping. That leaves only 25 percent of your time to actually do the work you enjoy. Although some projects may extend to as long as six months, a year, or even longer, you'll rarely feel you are a part of the organization. You'll always be an outsider. For managers and executives used to having their recommendations implemented with few questions, it can be a real shock when people spend good money for your advice and then ignore it! Your persuasive abilities will be critical to success, because if other people do not implement your recommendations, you cannot succeed.

In sum, consulting *is* a natural for people who like to work alone, who have a solid *self*-image, who have the financial security to carry them through establishing a practice, who have a professional image and reputation and a track record for handling tough issues.

Retirement

Long, lazy days stretching one after another; mornings on the deck reading the paper before heading for the golf course; time with the grandkids; gardening or reading in the hammock. Sounds good, doesn't it? When you have a full-time job, retirement sounds like an endless vacation.

Before you buy that rocking chair for the front porch, however, you might want to take a look at retirees in your community. They are probably the busiest people around. You'll find them enrolled in classes, earning new degrees, traveling, working, volunteering, running marathons, writing books, starting new businesses, mentoring young entrepreneurs, taking up oil painting, and surfing the Net. And yes, they're even playing golf; but after the first few months it's probably taking a backseat to other interests. "Retirement," wrote Stephen M. Pollack and Mark Levine in *Worth*," is a weird social experiment, a historical blip. Its collapse will be a triumph for common sense."

Planning for retirement may be the greatest challenge you'll ever face because the opportunities are vast. Let me first dispel the assumption that choosing retirement is irreversible. People who enter midlife career transition may well move in and out of "retirement" several times, reassessing needs and goals periodically, and adjusting their lives accordingly. Taking better care of themselves and living longer, healthier lives than previous generations, they will make plans "for life," rather than plans for retiring "from life."

A Commonwealth Fund Study in the early nineties showed that one-half of the total population over the age of seventy-five was involved in volunteer work. It also reported that 80 percent of people age fifty-five and older who were employed were also involved in volunteer activities. A Harris Poll in 1999 showed that 76 percent of retirees would like to be working and 86 percent opposed mandatory retirement. It also found that those over age sixty-five who were employed were "significantly" more satisfied with life than were those who were not. Planning for retirement should allow for changes in your lifestyle. Today's seniors are joining the Peace Corps, working with Habitat for Humanity, and volunteering their expertise to developing countries. Who knows where your path will lead? Deciding to retire doesn't mean stopping. It means choosing.

A Time to Grow Together

There's so much to think about during a career transition that it's easy to forget that people close to you are going through their own transitions. In fact, as you begin to gain confidence and direction, it may be somewhat unnerving to family and friends. You may be less accessible to them and probably not as predictable as they have come to expect. You will be a work in progress, so as you step off the beaten path and become a trailblazer, remember to pause occasionally to tell the story of your journey to loved ones. Whole new opportunities may open for you to evolve together and you may inspire them to become more adventurous in their own journeys.

Relationships, like most things in life, do not remain static. They grow or they die. Midlife career transitions can place incredible stress on close relationships, drawing people together or, all too often, driving them apart. Marriages, parent/child relationships, and friendships die more often from lack of attention and honest communication than they do from major crises, so pay close attention to yours.

Relationships can also be smothered by overconfidence. It is easy to assume we know what our loved ones think and believe instead of asking them. Find time for real conversation, someplace without distraction, for open-ended discussion, for listening that goes beyond words and reaches for understanding. Agree that there will be no assumptions and nothing will be beyond questioning as you create the future together.

It will help if you practice the five R's of active listening:

1. *Receive:* Listen with an open mind. Do not interrupt or interject with your own comments or lead conversations with interpreting phrases like "you mean . . ." Don't finish someone's sentences for them.

2. *Restate:* Did you understand what was just said? To be sure, paraphrase it in your own words. Make it very clear that you are seeking clarification, not merely repeating or judging what the other person said. It may be helpful to begin by saying, "What I am hearing you say is . . . Is that correct?" Welcome corrections to misconceptions.

3. *Reaffirm:* Make it clear that you value the person and their thoughts. Acknowledge that people may well have different opinions without thinking any less of each other. You may not agree, but hearing other viewpoints may clarify your own.

4. *Reflect:* Take time to consider what you've just heard before responding, particularly if you're on a touchy subject. Conversations about relationships should not be competitive or adversarial. Conversation is like encouraging a novice at Ping-Pong. Keep the ball moving, and instead of trying to outsmart the opponent or smash the ball, see how easy you can make it for them to return. This is one game best played to a draw.

5. *Respond:* Your job is to help the other person understand what you are saying. Don't give up until you are sure you have clearly expressed your thoughts. Don't demand an immediate response. Use time as a tool, not a weapon. Failing to respond in an appropriate amount of time can give the impression that you don't care; knee-jerk responses are ones you may soon regret.

Midlife is the time to dare to dream. Get rid of the "shoulds" and "can'ts" and "musts." Instead, speak and think in questions and "what-ifs."

It's important to communicate well with people close to you, but it's also important to set aside time to be alone with your own thoughts and feelings, to allow yourself to just "be." Take a quiet walk in the woods or by the ocean, where the enormous power of the sea makes everything in life seem somehow smaller and more manageable. Curl up on the sofa and watch the flames flicker in the fireplace. Wherever you are, however, find space for your thoughts. Commune with yourself. An unexpected midlife career transition disrupts life and it can throw you into survival mode. It can also place a significant strain on your sense of place in society and leave you feeling as though you are floating in space without a tether.

Trust in yourself and recognize that while our jobs fill an important place in our lives, they cannot be the center of our lives. Focus on becoming a "Master of Life," seeing this transition as a process that honors the past, delights in the present, and views the future as an unexplored world waiting to be discovered.

Life Masters are people who:

. . . trust their own instincts, intuitions, values, and abilities;

. . . welcome the approval of others, but don't need it;

. . . trust their own capabilities rather than seek protection;

. . . have a larger purpose in their lives than basic survival;

. . . dare to risk because they believe in themselves;

. . . don't spend their emotional energies on regrets or tri-fles;

. . . retain a sense of humor and perspective.

Midlife, indeed, is a time of options. It is a time to review and regroup, to dream new dreams and set new goals, to honor the power and freedom that come from knowing who we are. It is the time to recognize options, make choices, seek opportunities, and welcome the adventure. The Japanese have an interesting perspective on aging: The older we get, the heavier our obligation is to use the wisdom we have gained. How will *you* use the wisdom you've acquired?

CHAPTER THREE

Twelve Ground Rules Before You Begin the Job Search

> *"Work comes out of life, the way grass grows, the way apple trees 'apple.' Because human beings are active creatures, they naturally work."*
>
> —LAURENCE G. BOLDT, *Zen and the Art of Making a Living*

Is your age an advantage in a job search? It can be. To help you, I've developed twelve rules based on identifying and dealing with potential obstacles to success. Some relate to professional skills, others to job search expertise, and still others point directly to personal characteristics that can either help or hinder you when you're trying to make a good first impression. There are ways to deal with these obstacles . . . chiefly by becoming more aware of spoken or unspoken messages you're sending and making necessary adjustments. Beginning a job search without first tackling them is foolish.

Age bias looms large for someone at midlife. However the American Association of Retired Persons (AARP) has conducted numerous studies on the subject and they've found hiring managers believe there are important advantages to hiring older employees, including:

- in-depth experience, which leads to better judgment

- greater commitment to quality

- good communication skills; they get along well with co-workers

- loyalty to company goals

- strong work ethic

- highly developed skills and competencies

These same managers generally agree there can be disadvantages to hiring older employees, such as resistance to change, reluctance to accept and use new technology, a know-it-all attitude, and discomfort when they have to report to a younger manager. Few midlife career transitioners are ready for retirement, and although you may have difficulty accepting the fact that your age qualifies you for inclusion in AARP statistics, the results of these studies are worth considering.

Why defeat yourself before you begin? The old adage that you have only one opportunity to make a good first impression was never so true as in a midlife career transition, where preconceived notions meet you at the door. I am happy to say my clients in the following case studies were all eventually successful in their job searches, although some had a more difficult time than others. I hope their experiences will be helpful to you as you begin your own job search.

Rule # 1: Remember Your Age Is an Issue; It's Up to You to Make It an Advantage

CASE STUDY: Fred sat in front of me, nervously crossing one leg over the other again and again, his hands gesturing wildly as he told me he'd been looking for a job for more than seven months. Fred had been VP of international sales for a major company, but he'd been let go in a corporate shake-up. A six-figure income and a job that kept him traveling to major capitals of the world on a weekly basis had disappeared almost overnight when the new CEO brought in his own team.

Fred is intense, competitive, and completely unable to sit still for more than a few minutes. A picture right out of the pages of *GQ* magazine, he is the image of success, a deal maker who thrives on the chase, used to hammering out agreements, driving home the contract details, and then flying off to the next meeting.

Fred couldn't believe he hadn't been able to find a job. He had excellent contacts and an impressive network of people at high levels in corporations around the world. He was well known and well liked   and fifty-six years old. As we reviewed his search over the last weeks, his smile slowly faded, and for a moment he looked defeated as he asked, "Is it my age? Am I too old?"

If someone with Fred's flair was worried about his age keeping him from finding a job, it's no wonder age is the major concern of nearly everyone who loses a job at midlife. It's a valid concern in a youth culture such as ours, where products to make people look and feel younger crowd the shelves.

Older workers have been the primary victims of downsizing efforts over the last ten years. They hold mid- and upper-level management positions that are being eliminated and their salaries are high. They've been the first to go and the last to be rehired because potential employers see them as overqualified and overpriced. Some have taken early retirement, expecting to find jobs in short order, only to find that what started as choice has become enforced retirement.

Fred's solution: Fred's ego had gotten in the way of effective networking. His contacts were real; he knew people who could introduce him to decision makers at the highest levels, but he was reluctant to ask for help. Instead, he continued to glad-hand and enthusiastically talk about all the great opportunities he was considering (none of which really existed). It was getting him nowhere.

As a top salesman, Fred knew you can't make a sale unless you get to the right person. When I was able to convince him that a job search was another sales project, Fred began to make use of his extensive network, asking friends and associates for references, ideas, and emotional support. He was careful not to impose on social relationships, but when he met them for squash games and drinks after "work," he was more open about his career search. He stopped pretending. He began to ask for introductions at companies he was interested in and often was able to go directly to the CEO. His age was an asset because of the networking contacts he had made over the years. It wasn't long before he was, indeed, evaluating several offers.

Rule # 2: Think of Yourself As a Company of One

CASE STUDY: Pat didn't seem very concerned about his job loss. A mechanical engineer with several patents to his name, he had held various positions at gas and oil companies over the past thirty years, primarily in research and development. His last job was managing a team of engineers. He's brilliant, eccentric, and very opinionated. He wears trademark ties and matching suspenders in colors and patterns that make you wish you were wearing sunglasses on the cloudiest day. He has a disconcerting way of fixing people with a perplexed look when they make small talk, then responding with an amazing piece of natural-science trivia. Clearly, he has no time for chitchat.

Pat explained to me that he'd lost his job because the company had decided not to go forward with his last project, but that was okay, it wasn't very interesting anyway. Pat was going to look for another engineering job, but he wanted to be sure it would be working on a design team, not managing people. In the meantime, he thought he'd go ahead and get his Ph.D., because he might want to be a university engineering professor someday.

Pat grinned, told me he'd see me in a couple of days, and left my office. I looked forward to his return, because I knew right then that Pat would be one of my favorite clients.

People who find career transitions the easiest are the ones whose work is a part of who they are, and not just a job. They are the people who combine their natural talents with their interests and then build solid skills around them.

Pat's solution: Pat is an engineer, period. He will create and design, no matter where he works, no matter who employs him. He is the quintessential "company of one" who moves from company to company, taking his bag of tricks with him, doing a good job, and then moving on. He has a firm grip on his identity, never losing it to a company. His age is an advantage, not only because of his skills and experience, but because it simply is not part of his own consciousness. He is ageless.

Helping Pat was not so much a matter of counseling him through transition issues as developing a marketing strategy. Together, we identified consulting groups that could benefit from his background and skills, and created an effective portfolio. I spent a certain amount of time coaching him on interviewing, and helping him resist his impulse to go off on a tangent about the orbit of the planet Mars! By the way, Pat is also working on his Ph.D. and looking forward to becoming a university professor . . . when he has time.

Rule # 3: Be Prepared for an Extensive Job Search If You're Changing Fields

CASE STUDY: Phyllis walked into my office on her fiftieth birthday, full of anger, bitterness, frustration, and determination. My overall impression was of someone who was powerful and uncompromising. Her first words were, "I'm sick and tired of taking care of other people. I don't want to manage anybody ever again. I'm fifty and I've done it long enough. I'm going to do what I want to do for a change."

Obviously, she wasn't interested in my input at the moment, so I sat back and listened for an hour, interjecting a question now and then. Gradually, she began to slow down; her voice became less agitated; she relaxed back into her chair and finally laughed—a wonderful, melodious laugh—and said, "Guess I really needed that, huh?"

Phyllis had been in the financial investment business for twenty-five years, working for some of the best-known firms in the country. She could boast of a list of achievements anyone would be proud to claim. Her supervisors had been quick to note her commanding presence and authoritarian manner and consistently placed her in management positions, which she hated. She wanted to be wheeling and dealing with major corporate clients, not wasting her time (as she saw it) with underlings. At her fiftieth birthday, she saw her professional life slipping away without being able to do the work she enjoyed. When she arrived in my office, she had just abruptly resigned.

I took a deep breath and we began.

It's true. Some people choose to plunge into a midlife career transition, but very few have any idea what they are facing. Like Phyllis, most have been in the same career field all their lives, often with the same employer. They frequently have an unrealistic view of their marketability, and higher expectations than the market is likely to fulfill. Phyllis had no idea that she couldn't go right out and find a job within a few days. She was accustomed to success for good reason— she's smart and capable. But she should have done some research before quitting her job.

Phyllis's solution: Phyllis needed some reality therapy to help her understand the challenge she was facing and to get her started on the groundwork for a successful job search. First, I explained that the average search takes between four and six weeks for every $10,000 of salary you're seeking. Phyllis was making $125,000 a year, so it was entirely possible that it would take her a year to find a job at the same salary, perhaps more if she decided to leave management and build an investment clientele of her own. It was time for some hard decisions, but Phyllis was determined, a person with both the strength of character and the flexibility to go after what she wanted. She was willing to risk her savings to take time to find the right job.

We began with extensive self-assessment. Although Phyllis knew she didn't want to manage, she really didn't know why. We examined her communication style and explored her Personal Drivers (what motivated her, how she defined success, what energized her, what made her happy, and what was drudgery). We also talked about management styles, including her own, to determine if she had been expected to manage in a way that was incompatible with her natural style. The result was unequivocal: Phyllis much preferred to work with people who were her intellectual and professional equals. It was not managing, as such, that she disliked, but devoting most of her time to people who were just learning the business. Our task was clear: to look for positions at companies with a team culture or at consulting firms.

Phyllis became very enthused, and with her contacts and professional reputation, she landed a job ten months later with a very powerful investment consulting firm in New York. It was a good match. It will be a while before she rebuilds her investment portfolio, but that's fine with her. She's doing what she loves and it all happened because she took the time to know herself better in order to find a position that fit her Personal Profile.

Rule # 4: Do a Reality Check on Your Personal Communication Style

People who have worked for the same company for many years may not be aware that their communication style is a serious handicap in the job search. Companies can sometimes become like families; people get used to each other and excuse behaviors that would be unacceptable anywhere else. Coworkers learn to avoid difficult people, and as a result, the offenders never fully realize how abrasive their behavior is, much less learn to correct it. Only when they are forced out do these behaviors become serious handicaps. Such was the case with Helen.

CASE STUDY: Helen worked for a government agency for more than twenty years. She was an expert civil-rights attorney, as reliable as casebooks in recalling minute details of complicated proceedings. She was a critical resource to the organization and her work was her life.

Helen was also one of the most difficult people I've ever known. Abrupt and authoritarian, she was totally insensitive to other people. She burst into offices without knocking, barking orders left and right. Her voice was loud and strident, her raucous laughter and high-pitched tone making it nearly impossible for anyone to concentrate. In meetings, she alternated frantically doodling with noisily rifling through her briefcase.

Through the years supervisors and peers had tried to make Helen understand how disruptive her behavior was, and for a short time she would quiet down. But not for long. Eventually everyone gave up. Her last boss had eliminated staff meetings and relied on e-mail to communicate with his staff, as it was impossible to conduct a meeting with Helen present. She had been moved to an isolated office and used the steno pool for her clerical needs, as no administrative assistant would stay with her long. Helen's employer was a classic example of an organization that thinks of its members (dysfunctional as they might be) as part of a business family. Just like a real family, they put up with each other's idiosyncrasies and avoid touchy subjects.

In its own way, the organization limped along reasonably well. Helen made valuable contributions, developing her expertise and filling a vital role. It never occurred to her, or anyone else, that she would ever leave. Then the impossible happened. A new CEO came on board and took one short week to decide Helen's behavior was too great a price to pay for her expertise.

Helen's position was eliminated, her job responsibilities turned over to a consultant. She was devastated. And she faced a tremendous challenge. No one had ever really made it clear to her that what she was doing was wrong, or if they did, they had not followed through by insisting that she improve her behavior. Now in her early forties, she was nearly unmarketable. She had never accepted criticism, constructive or otherwise, and was in no mood to listen to it now. She hadn't been on the job market in twenty years; her communication skills made it impossible for her to make a good impression during an interview; she had nothing to fall back on except her expertise.

Helen's story is a tragic one. I'm sorry to say it is not unusual, except that Helen is an extreme. People like Helen never really grow up, for their work environment enables their bad habits and eventually handicaps them. Left on her own, she was nearly nonfunctional. The greatest favor family, friends, and coworkers can do for someone who is entering a job search is to provide a "reality check" of their communication style. It's not easy, of course. If you've ever been close to someone like Helen, you may be so used to odd behaviors that you don't recognize the seriousness of the problem. More importantly, you also don't want to hurt their feelings, particularly now when they've just lost their job.

Helen's solution: With Helen, I faced a serious challenge of my own. She didn't listen to managers who had attempted to counsel her in the past and she was convinced the only problem was that the new CEO didn't like her. Just talking about the situation was not going to get us anywhere. No one could "outtalk" Helen! So, I asked her to agree to what is called a "360-degree" review. I hoped this written set of evaluations would be more effective than trying to discuss the situation with her. She selected ten people for me to interview, including managers, coworkers, support staff, and professional associates outside the office. The interviews included an anonymous written questionnaire and personal interviews with open-ended questions designed to elicit subjective responses. I used the questionnaires to create an overall rating of her skills and then transcribed the oral feedback, all of which I reviewed with Helen. It was a difficult session for both of us, but the result was well worth it. Finally, she understood the reality and was ready to accept help.

I'd like to say everything went well after that, but it was a long process that tried the patience of both of us many times. She spent a lot of time working with a psychologist and a lot of time in our office, learning to be more aware of other people. She did have a sense of humor and that helped. Every now and then she would look at me with a twinkle in her eye and say, "I'm doing it again, huh?"

Eventually, Helen felt she was ready to look for another position and fortunately she was able to go back into the work she loved, where her expertise was so needed. This time she was determined to place more emphasis on work relationships and to become a positive influence in the office, rather than a disruptive one.

Rule #5: Take Time to Deal with the Pain of the Transition

Being forced to leave a company you love is a professional and emotional blow. Take the time to mourn this loss. You may even seek professional counseling if it begins to threaten your physical and emotional health. People who have been part of an organization for a long time are invested in the company and its product. They feel an ownership and responsibility for its welfare. When you've been an integral part of developing a product line, there is almost a physical pain, in addition to the emotional anguish, when you're torn from your "parental" role.

CASE STUDY: Sandy was a program director for a biomedical research company. At age fifty-six, she had been in the field for more than thirty years, with the same company for sixteen years, and researching the same project for seven years. The news that the FDA had finally approved the product became bittersweet when she learned funds for future research were gone. The company had decided to divert those funds into new product marketing. At her greatest moment of success, her job was over. The leave-taking was heartbreaking.

Sandy, gentle and soft-spoken, came into my office in rumpled blue jeans and a starched white lab coat. Her eyes were a piercing steel blue that lit up when she talked about her work. A widow, she lived alone, spending long hours in the lab, her real home since her husband's death. Cleaning the lab equipment and packing it all away had taken a couple of weeks, but now she had to face the future. She had never looked for a job, never written a résumé. A California-based company had called and was interested in her, but she just wasn't sure she wanted to move so far away.

Poised and confident in her lab, Sandy was insecure and frightened on the job search. Going back over thirty years of work to write accomplishment statements was one of the hardest things she'd ever done, and we spent long hours on interviewing skills before she felt comfortable talking about herself. The idea of beginning again was a major hurdle, a large part of which was her fear of becoming attached to another project only to be forced out again. She didn't think she could go through it again.

The loss of a job is a major life crisis because a job is so much more than a job; it's a social system, a place where you belong, the place where you do meaningful work. When it ends, you invariably mourn for a dream that is over.

Sandy's solution: Sandy wasn't ready to look for another job or to interview with a potential new employer until she had put her last work experience in perspective and some of the pain had diminished. She wasn't ready to deal with emotionally charged questions like, "Why did you leave your last position?"

We spent many hours together, during which she came to grips with the reality that she couldn't go back to her old lab. What she did have, however, was the high regard and enthusiastic support of people she had worked with and they were more than ready to steer her to new possibilities. She needed time to heal before she moved forward. When she did, she focused on the future with energy and enthusiasm. Sandy is a very special person. Her new employer recognized her strengths immediately and placed her in charge of the lab.

Rule # 6: Learn the Job Search Process Before You Begin

Highly competent people are often surprised to discover how hard it can be to find a new position. They don't realize it's a process that requires time, dedicated attention, and often professional help. Don't lose valuable time and viable prospects or risk serious damage to your self-confidence by muddling through the job search. There's a better way. The adage that "a lawyer who represents himself in court has a fool for a client" might well be applied to someone who enters a job search without professional help. Mark was just such a case.

CASE STUDY: Mark had been the CFO of a major national retail chain. When he came to me, he had been out of work for fifteen months. In that time he had been a finalist for ten top jobs in the United States and Canada. He was convinced that someone at his old company was blackballing him when prospective employers called for references, and he wanted to take legal action to put a stop to it.

Mark is a tall, handsome, rather elegant man with great presence. A trifle condescending, he is obviously used to being in charge. He's eminently qualified and personally impressive. My challenge was to determine what had been keeping him from landing a job. I thought it highly unlikely bad references were killing Mark's chances. My experience has shown that when companies fire someone, they just want them out of there. They are not trying to settle a blood feud.

We began by analyzing the jobs Mark had come close to capturing, and I learned that all of them had come through headhunters. As we researched each situation, I realized that all but three had been looking for a candidate with a major qualification Mark was missing, such as experience with Canadian tax laws, SEC dealings, or high-tech financing. Mark brushed this aside, peremptorily telling me number crunching is the same, regardless of the industry. Over and over, as I pointed out qualifications he was missing, he pooh-poohed them, restating his belief that he was being blackballed.

Finally, we looked at the three cases where he seemed perfectly suited for the position. I began to review his résumé and was amazed to see the difference between the confident, professional person in front of me and the decidedly unprofessional résumé that was supposed to represent him.

Mark's solution: First, I had to convince Mark how very important a well-developed résumé is to a successful career transition. It is the major marketing piece. He was reluctant at first to spend the thirty to forty hours it would take to develop a comprehensive written record of his professional history. Probably the deciding factor was when I gently told him my suspicion that he had never been seen as a serious candidate. You see, headhunters must present a minimum number of qualified candidates to companies for review. Mark had the background and the personal presence to represent them well, but they were no doubt using him as the comparison, rather than the lead candidate, because his résumé gave them so little to go on. I reminded Mark that the winner in a job search is not the person who has the most interviews, but the person who gets the one right interview.

It was also important for Mark to carefully review his

work experience and be able to talk about it in a convincing manner, rather than just assume a list of his past positions spoke for him. The intense process of developing the résumé is probably more important for this reason than any other. For Mark, the next few months were life changing. He began to better understand himself and why he had been successful in the past. His defensive arrogance transformed into real confidence. Instead of looking for someone to blame, he began to realize that it was up to him to take charge of his career. When he began a new position four months later, he thanked me, not only for the counseling, but for helping him become, as he said, "a person I like better." I liked him better, too.

People who go through a midlife career transition rarely come out the other side unchanged. It's a rite of passage that few enjoy, but most say they're glad they experienced.

Rule # 7: Don't Compete with Thirty-Five-Year-Olds; Let Them Compete with You

Traditional wisdom says that it's harder to find a job if you are a senior executive or have many years of experience. Obviously, there are fewer jobs at the top of the pyramid. What no one tells you is that there are also fewer people looking for them, so in reality it all evens out. Your competition will be people at higher levels who are willing to take a cut in title and salary, or people at lower levels who are on the way up. In most cases, this latter category will be younger than you are. They will be willing to work for up to 30 percent less than you made at your last job. They may also appear to have more energy and enthusiasm.

Your first inclination may be to go out and get the graduate or undergraduate degree you never completed. Forget it. It's not going to get you a job. You're past that stage. Degrees provide the academic preparation to launch a career, but they are less impressive than accomplishments that demonstrate your capabilities in real terms. The reality is that you *can* get the degrees; the thirty-five-year-old *cannot* get experience comparable to yours without putting in the time, so fight this battle on *your* turf.

> **CASE STUDY:** Jim was a human-resources manager for more than twenty-four years. He started out as an accounting clerk in payroll, but over the years his people skills consistently earned him promotions. He was even recruited by other companies as his expertise in labor negotiations grew.
>
> Jim is a pleasant man, with a deceptively mild manner. He smiles easily and always appears relaxed, speaking quietly and listening attentively. He dresses tastefully and it's hard to ignore his marathon runner's build. He is not a forceful person, although there is a firmness in his voice that tells me he is confident in his own views.
>
> Jim doesn't have a bachelor's degree in human resources or any related field, although he takes courses specifically related to his work and he does have an HR Certificate. When his job ended in the wake of an acquisition, he quickly noticed job openings at his level invariably asked for at least a bachelor's degree, and often a master's. When he came to me, he was very discouraged and was considering enrolling in a degree program at a local university.

What Jim, and others like him, don't realize is that they don't need degrees to qualify them to do work they've already proven they can handle. Academic programs provide the foundation, the minimum knowledge required to embark on a career. As a result, recruiters generally establish a minimum academic requirement in order to ensure a basic standard. Don't be intimidated by a degree requirement or fail to apply for the position if your experience shows you have the skills for it.

Jim's solution: Jim needed to deal with the person who would be his direct manager. Invariably, that person is much more interested in experience than academic background. The key was for him to present his credentials in person rather than mailing in a résumé and job application and risking being screened out by a lower-level human-resource employee.

We made two lists: one of companies that could use his labor union experience in the building trades, and one of people he had met over the years who had either worked for these companies or provided services to them, such as vendors, accountants, and attorneys. He called each one to set up meetings to explain what he was looking for and ask them to make initial contacts for him. Because of his age and experience, they felt confident in doing so. The decision makers also knew this wasn't a casual networking call, and regardless of whether or not they had an opening at the time, they knew they could expect to learn something from Jim. Meeting him was worth their time.

Rule # 8: Become Computer Literate

One of the clear-cut findings of the Harris Poll commissioned by the AARP study is the perception that older workers are not technologically competent. This can be a major handicap to finding employment. Executives who are used to having secretaries handle their correspondence soon learn companies are no longer willing to provide this kind of personal assistance; they will be expected to handle their own support functions. The ability to handle a variety of software tools is a basic requirement for almost any position. Using e-mail is not a convenience; it's a necessity.

CASE STUDY: Howard is a fifty-five-year-old manufacturing manager. Downsized from a company two years ago, he spent almost a year on the job search before he finally found a great opportunity to direct the move of a manufacturing facility from one state to another. He worked fourteen-hour days six days a week for six months, completing the job on time and under budget. He had fully expected to continue as operations manager of the new site.

Everything went well for about three months. One day, he was called in to the human-resource director's office and asked why he didn't use e-mail. Howard replied that he had always believed in talking to people in person and couldn't see much sense in sending mail to someone in the next office. He was told the CEO wanted everyone to communicate through e-mail, as it was more efficient and took the place of staff meetings. Howard agreed to rely more on e-mail, and for a while he did. Gradually, however, he went back to his old ways. Two months later he was once again called into the HR director's office and told he was being let go. Confidentially, the director explained that his unwillingness to use e-mail was the reason. The CEO felt he was not functioning as part of the team and attributed it to his age and inflexibility.

CASE STUDY: Sonja was fifty-eight when she lost her mid-level management position. She agreed to take on a short-term project for another company, hoping it would turn into a full-time position. However, the first week she was there, she brought a lengthy handwritten memo to the administrative assistant and asked her to type it up and distribute it. The assistant pleasantly told her that everyone did their own correspondence, but she would be happy to show her how to use the word-processing program, if she needed help. Sonja stormed out of the room, saying, "I'm not a secretary. I don't type." Needless to say, she didn't last long enough to complete the project.

Unfortunately, the assumption that people of a certain age may be reluctant to learn to use computers is borne out by reality much too often. There are people out there like Sonja who regard using them a support-level function. They are unwilling to spend the time and energy to become competent, or perhaps are afraid of computers. Whether it's using e-mail, project management tools, handling your own correspondence, researching, downloading, or using the Internet or Lotus Notes, it is essential to be fully functional and independent, able to use the information systems that are integral to every company. The first item of business for anyone in midlife career transition should be to recognize this fact and do what is necessary to become proficient. Remember, recruiters and hiring managers may assume you are incompetent because of your age, even if you were on the technology advisory board at your last company! It is essential to let them know your capabilities.

Howard's and Sonja's solutions: The solutions were easy in these cases. They had both learned lessons the hard way before they came to me and were ready and willing to face the technology challenge. Howard got his own laptop and has become a whiz on the Internet. For Sonja, word processing is a useful tool, but she'll probably never really enjoy working with computers.

Our next task was to help them both incorporate their new skills into their résumés. We also discussed ways to respond in interview situations in order to show their newfound expertise and willingness to learn. Finally, we recast their accomplishments to show flexibility, adaptability, and innovation. In the end they both found new positions.

Rule # 9: Know Yourself and Where You Want to Go Before You Begin the Journey

Midlife career transition is a gift that forces us to take time out from the everyday business of life. Abruptly ejected from our familiar routines, suddenly the hours in the day stretch endlessly before us. In-boxes are gone. The alarm clock no longer interrupts our sleep. Like a train derailed, our journey has come to a halt.

As you face the future and recognize that "who" and "what" you are is no longer encapsulated in a specific job title at a particular company, you start to appreciate that you have the freedom to make choices. This is a beginning.

What an incredible opportunity! The saddest people I meet are the ones who reach retirement years only to realize that they never really enjoyed their work. They look back with regrets and "what ifs" that leave them feeling empty and unfulfilled. Life just happened to them. Darren is a classic example.

CASE STUDY: Darren entered my office with the flair of an actor taking center stage. He swept off his Australian outback hat and coat and gracefully eased into a chair. He was hardly what I was expecting of someone who had just accepted early retirement from a major national accounting firm. I had anticipated a person more reserved and certainly less flamboyant.

As we began to go over his program and discuss the options he had been offered, he became more and more withdrawn. Fascinated by his change in demeanor, I stopped referring to his work and retirement plans and asked him about his interests outside of work. Sure enough, he was a big fan of the theater, and before long he began to tell me about his long-abandoned dream of becoming an actor.

The son of an accountant, Darren had been encouraged by his

father to get a "real" job. He had become quite proficient in his work, but as he looked back on it, it all seemed so dull. He wondered where the time had gone.

Darren's solution: As we worked together over the next weeks, I encouraged him to take some classes and to audition for summer stock theater productions at a nearby resort. That was the first step. Several months later he took over as the administrative manager of a local theater. At least he's in a field he loves. Next, he's hoping to be up there on stage.

Unfortunately, a lesson we learn very young is that it is more important to get a job, to be doing *something*, than to enjoy what we are doing. At midlife, you can begin again, this time doing it *your* way.

Rule # 10: Learn the "Group Speak" of the Marketplace

To be credible applicants, job seekers must be familiar with current terminology and management theories, whether it's TQM (Total Quality Management), Just in Time, Process Flow, or Employee Empowerment. The list goes on and on, but the point is to spend some time in the business section of your local library. Managers should be able to define their own philosophy of management and evaluate the pros and cons of current styles. Other job seekers should understand the intricacies of teams and self-directed workforces and know where their own work style is the most effective. Interviews are no longer one-sided affairs, with the interviewer controlling the questions and making judgments on the answers. They are dialogues, and the applicant who cannot hold his/her own is at a disadvantage. It simply is not acceptable in today's marketplace to be less than savvy about the key players and terminology of the corporate world. Recent graduates of business programs may have an advantage here, but older workers can certainly acquire the knowledge with a little research.

> **CASE STUDY:** Myron was a senior manager who had worked out-side of the U.S. for the last seventeen years, first in the military and then as a civilian with the United Nations. Neither organization gave him a great deal of exposure to current management theories. His erect posture, authoritarian stride, and definitive statements left little doubt he was used to wearing a uniform that announced his rank, hardly the attitude preferred by most organizations, which are busy eliminating layers of authority.
>
> Much to his credit, he agreed to a regimen of three books a week as part of a crash course on corporate America. I assured him he need not agree with any of the authors, but he did need to become familiar with their ideas, and be able to discuss his own beliefs in comparison to them.

Myron's solution: Myron became informed, if not converted. He learned that his major job search challenge would be to find a company where his own style would mesh with the company culture. His energy and his confidence regained, he took charge of the search, determined to win.

Assuming that every company operates the way we're used to is a common problem for mid-age job seekers. It's a dangerous assumption for both the search *and* the transition into the new organization. Unfortunately, the concern of hiring managers that older workers will be inflexible has a great deal of basis in fact. They expect candidates over forty to be locked into old ways of doing things, unwilling to learn or even consider new methods, and even incapable of change. If you can discuss current thinking in an interview, it dispels these assumptions and opens the door for serious consideration.

Rule # 11: Develop a Career Transition Plan and Follow It

Finding a job is a full-time job, perhaps the most challenging you will ever undertake. Not just any job will do; your life is too important to waste on doing something you don't enjoy, and it is unlikely you will be successful if the job doesn't emphasize your talents. All of our lives we're told to work on our weaknesses, as though we are expected to be good at everything. Instead, focus on the things you do well, for they no doubt reflect your natural abilities.

The goal of a midlife career transition should be to find a job where you will be doing what you do best 80 percent of the time, where you are the most energized and time flies because you are enjoying what you are doing. It's reasonable to assume you will have to spend up to 20 percent of your time on tasks you might not enjoy but that nevertheless must be done. You'll find the ideal job by developing a thorough profile of it and then planning your campaign to find it. It won't be easy, and along the way you'll be tempted to take second best, but with a clear goal, a concrete plan, and a willingness to work at it full-time, you can look forward to success. Nothing else is good enough.

CASE STUDY: Bob was director of financial analysis for a major utility company when the company was sold off and moved to another state. Tall, slim, and polite, he was the perfect company man. He was at work no later than six-thirty in the morning and he was the last to leave at night. Unfailingly courteous, he also met every deadline and produced quality work that exceeded the most stringent requirements. The morning after his severance agreement was signed, Bob was waiting when I arrived at the office, dressed in a dark suit, white shirt, and regimental tie. His shoes had a mirror shine. I showed him to his desk, explained the resources available to him, and made an appointment to meet with him that afternoon. We had just established a daily routine that he would follow for the next six months. He was always waiting for me in the morning, and he always left when I did, long after five. He dressed professionally every day and never failed to put in at least an eight-hour day at "work."

Bob's solution: Bob's job search was not easy, and I am sure there were times when he would much rather have been skiing with his two teenage children than job hunting, but he never lost focus. His job, his goals for himself, and the expertise he had gained were not something he was willing to compromise. Although his high salary and the narrowness of his experience limited his opportunities, he also knew that the depth of his experience could not be matched by very many others, and he was determined to meet his goals.

We worked together very closely, analyzing potential companies and positions, developing strategies to present his qualifications, honing interview skills, and doing extensive research so he would be well informed on the current market. A large part of his success was due to the businesslike approach he took to his job search. This not only resulted in an excellent position, but it helped him to keep up his energy and confidence, one of the biggest challenges anyone faces in a career transition. When he succeeded, he was as convinced as I was that it had all been worth it. I chuckled, however, when I came to work the day after he had accepted his new position to see him waiting for me at the door, this time dressed in blue jeans and a denim shirt, both carefully pressed. I said, "Why, Bob, you have a job now, you don't have to be here." He smiled and replied, "I always like to be sure a job is finished properly. I thought I'd come in to close my files, and then write letters of appreciation to all of the people who helped me. I hope it's all right that I came dressed casually." A gentleman to the end.

Bob's approach might differ significantly from yours, but it was the right one for him, because it fit his style. A job search does need your full attention in order to build momentum, and that's true for everyone.

Rule #12: Create a Support Group for Your Search

As you move through this transition, everyone around you—family, friends, and associates—will be affected by your situation and, to varying degrees, will be wandering around in their own gray fog until you are launched in your new career path. There are various support groups available, some highly organized and some very informal, but the important thing is to talk to others who are going through the same experience. You may feel a tremendous sense of isolation when you leave a company, and it helps to know you're not alone. It is also reassuring to see that there are plenty of other talented, successful, highly qualified, marketable individuals who are out of work at the moment . . . just like you.

A support group also provides networking opportunities and a resource for evaluating job offers and brainstorming answers to difficult interview questions. There will be times when your energies, physical and emotional, are drained, and that's the time when your support group will be there to give you perspective and send you on your way again.

CASE STUDY: Brenda was terribly embarrassed when she lost her job. The last thing she wanted was to talk to anyone, much less to join a group of other people in the same situation. She avoided her friends and even stopped going to church. When she came to my office, she made a point of arriving just in time for her appointment in order to avoid my other clients.

She conscientiously completed her self-assessment exercises and finished her résumé in record time, determined to find another position immediately. However, she was reluctant to spend time researching the companies, and without networking contacts, her applications were getting little attention. In spite of my reassurances, she became more and more discouraged.

Brenda's solution: The turning point came when I convinced her to go to a client support session. She saw other people with impressive qualifications who were looking for jobs and she felt less isolated. She observed the practical application of the networking process and it wasn't long before she was back at church talking to people about her job search. A short time later she found a new position.

Midlife is a difficult time to be without a job. Most people want to work, regardless of age or financial status, and when a job ends unexpectedly, it's a devastating blow. Your age can be an advantage (or a disadvantage) depending upon how you handle the issue. If you are aware of the market, understand the preconceptions that may be out there, honestly evaluate your own strengths and weaknesses, and sincerely believe in the value you bring to a prospective employer, you're bound to be a winner!

CHAPTER FOUR

Assessing Your Career Interests

"Cowardice asks the question, 'Is it safe?'
Expediency asks the question, 'Is it politic?'
Vanity asks the question, 'Is it popular?'
But conscience asks the question, 'Is it
right?' "

—MARTIN LUTHER

I T's not about getting a job; it's about getting a life. Life is multifaceted, each facet integral to the whole, all interdependent. The challenge is to find balance so that work and play sustain and enrich each other.

For many, the struggle for survival has been replaced by a chase after mythical abundance, which always moves just out of reach. People at midlife are apt to be victims of a monster they themselves have created. Social status, security, the right house in the right neighborhood (much too large now that the children have gone), and the right vacations (to recover from the twelve-to-fourteen-hour workdays) are expectations they fear they will no longer be able to afford. They are often dismayed when I tell them a woman who reaches age fifty without cancer or heart disease can expect to live to ninety-two. Instead of joy, they're overcome with the added burden of making more money for retirement. What's wrong with this picture?

It's time to see the big picture and put life in perspective. Work is essential, but so is caring for our environment, learning to live together with respect and honor, and valuing the psychological and spiritual aspects of our lives as much as the economic and material.

As midlife career transitioners, we are the children of World War II parents and Depression-era grandparents, and our lives were heavily influenced by the fear and lack of control over life that they felt. To have a job, to be able to support ourselves and our families, to provide for our old age, not to be dependent upon anyone or anything else—we were taught that these values were far more important than enjoying life. Visible symbols of success reaffirm the control we exert over our lives. We stockpile them as insurance. When our jobs end, we feel very vulnerable.

For too many people, life is a series of problems to be solved rather than a thing of wonder to be explored. Analysis supplants faith; practical is more important than beautiful. "To think" has credibility; "to feel" is considered weak.

Midlife is a time to stop and question whether we are really on the right track, whether the values that dominate our lives are really the most important. A career transition is an opportunity to step off the path you're on and question where you are going and why. Remember the old Peggy Lee song "Is That All There Is?" The answer is to find your Life's Work, work that naturally flows from your talents, interests, and values, work that energizes you and makes you feel fulfilled, not merely a job that pays the bills for things you really don't need or want.

Life Balance

We hear so much these days about balance of life, as though there were some prescription for creating equilibrium. But if life is ever-evolving, then the right balance today may be wrong tomorrow. Do we feel this yearning for balance in our lives quite simply because we aren't listening to ourselves and honoring what really is important to us?

We aren't always able to choose how we spend our time, our energy, and our resources, but the enforced "time-out" of a midlife career transition creates an opportunity to manage the third third of our lives with conscious awareness and to readjust the balance of life.

▣ BALANCE-OF-LIFE PIE CHART

Create a Pie Chart that shows the amount of time and energy you typically devote to each of the following:

Mind: Learning, knowledge, problem solving, analyzing.
Body: Caring for your physical health: nutrition, exercise, wellness.
Spirit: Meaning and mission in life, sense of well-being, values, identity, and spirituality.
Relationships: Developing and nurturing supportive relationships with family, friends, and associates.

Career: Making a living and satisfying the need to be productive, to contribute.

Play: Rest, recreation, leisure activities that refresh and renew.

■   ■   ■

Take a look at the chart you've just created. Is this what you want your life to be? Is it optimally balanced for your needs and well-being? Of course, there are times when one aspect of your day-to-day life dominates. For example if you return to school, you'll spend a great deal of time in the classroom and studying. Similarly, a prolonged illness, yours or a member of your family's, will force you to focus on physical well-being. The pieces of the pie will seldom be equal, but if they are not, the mix should reflect your conscious decision.

Is your current career a plus or minus in this equation? Did spending a disproportionately large percentage of your time and energies on your career precipitate your current career transition? Remember, your career consumes the majority of your waking hours. If the work you choose doesn't include a significant portion of the other elements of your life (i.e., it doesn't challenge you mentally or drains you physically), it's impossible to maintain balance. If a job offer doesn't support your ideal life balance, what are the trade-offs? Are you willing to make them?

What is *your* ideal Life Balance? Nearly all of my midlife clients tell me that their demanding careers have been so much the focus of their lives that they have given limited time to relationships, physical health, and mental well-being and practically none to spirit or play. The surprising thing is how many say their jobs have not challenged their minds. The lucky ones had employers who provided health and on-site child-care facilities where they were able to spend time with their children during the day. Others emphasized training and education that stimulated them intellectually. Perhaps the greatest change clients tell me they plan to make next time is to reserve their evenings and weekends for family and, yes, to start that exercise program they've been talking about for so long. The important point is to make these choices a priority and find a job in a company that supports them.

▣ CREATE YOUR FUTURE BALANCE OF LIFE

What do you want your balance of life to be? Create a pie chart that shows how much of your time and energy you want to spend on each of these elements: Mind, Body, Career, Spirit, Play, and Relationships. Use it to evaluate potential jobs.

■　　■　　■

Enjoying the Work You Do

Probably the most important part of self-assessment is identifying what you really liked and disliked about previous jobs. Job satisfaction is more than pride in accomplishments, the tasks you do, or the skills you develop. It is more often determined by your compatibility with the culture and people with whom you interact.

This next exercise helps you review your career and think very specifically about what you liked and what you disliked. Don't be surprised if salary, benefits, or even the actual task you were doing doesn't top your list of likes. Very often, it's your relationship with a boss, your level of autonomy, or even the variety of your assignments. I've even had people tell me the thing they liked most was having an office window, so don't worry about whether the items on your list might seem trivial to someone else. If it matters to you, it's important. A great part of job satisfaction is whether or not you felt you "had a life," or just a job.

When it comes to dislikes, the same few items top many lists: being micromanaged, traveling more than half the time, repetitive work assignments, lack of communication, and unclear direction within the company. What were yours?

Consider the following as you complete the likes-and-dislikes worksheet that follows:

- Did you feel a sense of belonging? Did you think of your coworkers as your kind of people, your clan, your tribe?

- Did they share the same values? Did you laugh at the same jokes?

- How would you describe the management style?

- How were decisions made? Who was involved?

- Was maintaining the status quo important or were people always looking for new ways of doing things?

- Did seniority determine how your opinions were valued? Was the company more hierarchical or more entrepreneurial? Which are you? Was there a fit?

- Were there opportunities for growth? Career advancement?

- Did you have the equipment and resources you needed to do a good job?

- What was the style of dress?

- Were you proud of the product or service your company provided?

- How would you rate the compensation-and-benefit package?

- How would you describe the work environment?

- Were you expected to travel? How often? Under what conditions?

▣ LIKES & DISLIKES

LIKES	DISLIKES

Most Recent Position:

_____   _____

_____   _____

_____   _____

_____   _____

Prior Position:

_____   _____

_____   _____

_____   _____

_____   _____

Previous Positions:

_____   _____

_____   _____

_____   _____

_____   _____

Patterns: List below likes and dislikes that cropped up in more than one position.

_____   _____

_____   _____

_____   _____

_____   _____

Values: A Personal Line in the Sand

Conscience, the voice within; whatever you call it, it's the line you draw in the sand, the one you will not cross. It's the value system that frames your important decisions. It's why some things just seem right and others seem very wrong, an instinct that warns of danger and quietly applauds appropriate choices. Life gets so hectic that we must rely on this voice, because there never seems to be time for thinking deeply when a question arises. A midlife career transition provides the opportunity for reflecting on broader issues that make life meaningful.

We are influenced from birth by cultural values, those truths that our society holds dear: the laws that make it possible for people to interact with minimal conflict, the way culture perpetuates itself from generation to generation. For example, a cultural value in the United States is universal education, while in some societies education is restricted by class or the ability to pay for it. Our Constitution incorporates the basic tenets of our society, but there are other values that we assume, as though they were written in law, such as the frontier ethic, which respects bravery, independence, physical strength, honor, and competence with nature's vagaries. Most of us hold beliefs that are particular to the society into which we are born. It is difficult for us to escape ethnocentrism, judging other societies by the standards of our own. Our culture is our frame of reference. When we are functioning well within our society, we have a pretty clear idea when the things we do or think are acceptable to people around us.

Our personal values are greatly influenced by our cultural values and by our society, but they also owe a great deal to our families, our place within them, and to our own experiences. They stem from our fears and our weaknesses at least as often as from our strengths. They are certainly shaped by role models (both positive and negative), talents that are valued and rewarded, and even the jokes we hear growing up. What is mocked? What is revered? Whether or not we feel worthy to lead others is one of the dominating forces in career development. What are the messages that play over and over in our minds? How do they influence our decisions? How do we know when what we are hearing is inaccurate, something we have assumed to be true without ever testing it?

Over all are the universal values. The myths and legends of all societies bear an astonishing resemblance to one another. Recognizing the values that mold your life is helpful in developing clear career goals and identifying what motivates you professionally as well as personally. For example: Is making a great deal of money important to you? How about stability, a pension plan, a golden parachute, a contract that guarantees employment for a specific period of time? How important is geographic location? What about the time you'll have to spend with your family? Are status, respect, recognition, perks, and symbols of success top priorities for you? How about power and control? Or perhaps you would rather not be in charge and prefer to contribute quietly while someone else calls the shots and takes responsibility?

Your values may shift somewhat over time, but basic internal motivators tend to remain the same. A significant difference between external goals and your values creates internal conflict that sooner or later needs to be resolved. Such disparity may mean that you are putting other people's demands or needs ahead of your own. Do your family, spouse, friends, or boss expect something of you that really isn't important to you? Is their approval more important to you than anything else? Or are you primarily determined to avoid conflict? Are you on a track you'd rather jump? That's the great part of midlife career transition; you're driving this train.

What Is Important to You?

What values mean the most to you? Use these questions to begin a personal dialogue. What choices will you make based on your values? Where do you draw *your* "line in the sand"?

▣ UNIVERSAL VALUES

1. What is your mission in life?

_____

_____

2. How would you like to be remembered when you are gone?

_____

_____

_____

3. What is your proudest achievement?

_____

_____

4. Make a list of the five things you value most.

_____

_____

_____

_____

_____

▣ CULTURAL VALUES

1. When you were a child, what made you proudest? When was your family most likely to praise you? To be disappointed in you?

_____

_____

_____

_____

2. What role did community service or religion play in your life?

_____

_____

_____

3. How did you relate to friends, teachers, your family, other adults in
the community?

_____

_____

_____

_____

_____

4. When you were a child, what did you dream of becoming? What did
you imagine your life would be? What were your goals? How have they
changed throughout life?

_____

_____

_____

_____

_____

_____

5. What was the most traumatic event of your childhood? How did it affect your life?

_____

_____

_____

_____

▣ Personal Values

1. What is your definition of integrity? How important is it to you in choosing friends? In choosing employers?

_____

_____

_____

2. What are the characteristics you most admire in others? In yourself?

_____

_____

3. What embarrasses you? Touches you? Amuses you? Excites you? Frightens you? Makes you happy?

_____

_____

_____

_____

4. What role does your work play in your life?

_____

_____

_____

_____

5. Is there anything or anyone for which you would give your life?

_____

_____

6. If you could give one gift or one piece of advice to everyone in the world, what would it be? Why?

_____

_____

_____

_____

7. What is the most important lesson you have learned in life? How does it affect the decisions you make?

_____

_____

_____

_____

■ ■ ■

There are no right or wrong answers to these questions. They are, however, an important part of finding your life's work, and for recognizing it when you do.

What Makes a Job Satisfying to You?

Discovering your life's work is a search that starts within. It is consciously matching your values, interests, and talents with work that needs doing. "Getting a job" has always had a negative connotation. It's something you do because you must. It's all tied up with that "real life" concept that says adult life is burdened with responsibility and duty, rather than being a time of self-fulfillment. I encourage you to approach your career transition as an opportunity to understand the elements of a job that enhance your ability to be who and what you are and then look for jobs to match these.

In the next exercise, rate the value you place on each criterion for job satisfaction and then prioritize them.

▣ CRITERIA FOR JOB SATISFACTION

Place an *X* in the column that best describes the extent to which you value each item.

	Very	**Somewhat**	**Less**
Salary	_____	_____	_____
Benefits	_____	_____	_____
Promotion Potential	_____	_____	_____
Decision-making Authority	_____	_____	_____
Responsibilities	_____	_____	_____
Leadership/Supervision	_____	_____	_____

	Very	Somewhat	Less
Work Relationships	_____	_____	_____
Variety	_____	_____	_____
Autonomy	_____	_____	_____
Challenge	_____	_____	_____
Learning/Growth Opportunities	_____	_____	_____
Prestige/Title	_____	_____	_____
Schedule/Flexibility	_____	_____	_____
Size of Company	_____	_____	_____
Product and Quality	_____	_____	_____
Environmental Concern	_____	_____	_____
Industry	_____	_____	_____
Physical Environment	_____	_____	_____
Geographic Location	_____	_____	_____
Corporate Image/Integrity	_____	_____	_____
People/Culture/Style	_____	_____	_____
Stability/Economic Security	_____	_____	_____
Flexibility for Family Time	_____	_____	_____
Recognition	_____	_____	_____
Contribution/Service to Society	_____	_____	_____
Physical/Mental Health/ Quality of Life	_____	_____	_____
Leisure Time	_____	_____	_____
Self-Expression/Creativity	_____	_____	_____
Travel	_____	_____	_____

Prioritize the five which are most important to you:

1. _____

2. _____

3. _____

4. _____

5. _____

■   ■   ■

Talents: Your Natural Bliss

Everyone is born with talents. They are the original birthday presents, the most valuable gifts we ever receive. Yet many people go through life without ever opening them or even realizing they exist.

Skills can be developed with a great deal of determination and effort (yours or someone else's!), but skills built on natural talents come easily. When you combine skills and talents with vision and purpose, you find your life's work. Suddenly everything comes together; you are of one piece. While we do nothing to deserve the talents we are given, there nevertheless is an obligation to recognize them, develop them, and use them well. If you take a cosmic view of life, it's easy to imagine that talents were distributed in a logical manner, like the pieces of a great puzzle. We each have a duty to find our piece and add it to the puzzle of humankind.

You are no doubt using your natural talents when you feel the most content, the most fulfilled, when you lose track of time because you're enjoying yourself so much. A natural talent is so easy for you that it's hard to understand why other people have any trouble with it. Imagine a world of work based on your natural talents.

Finding Your Natural Talents

Sometimes it's difficult to recognize your natural talents. It helps to consider the following questions.

1. When you were a small child, what were you most often doing when you lost track of time?

2. What subject was easiest for you in school?

3. When were people most likely to say, "You're so good at . . ." or "It's so easy for you"?

4. What are the activities at your work that you find the most satisfying? What role do you typically fill in a group activity? What do other people rely on you to provide? How does it reflect your natural talents?

5. If you didn't need the money, what "work" would you do just because it's fun?

6. In your home and personal life, what do other people enjoy most about you? What talent is it?

7. What makes you the most irritable? What do you dislike doing the most? What do you hate to be responsible for? What do you try to avoid or do last? How does this reflect something you definitely do not have any talent in, regardless of skill?

8. When are you happiest? Why?

9. When are you the most confident? The most creative? The most untroubled by risks?

10. When do you like yourself best?

Defining Your Purpose and Mission

Midlife just happens. Suddenly you realize (or your teenager reminds you!) that you're nearly half a century old and it dawns on you that you don't have as many years ahead of you as you have left behind. Mortality raises its ugly head. Never mind that you could get run over by a truck at any moment, there's something comforting about expecting life to go on for a long, long time. Then you're fifty and everything changes.

You become aware of little things. You notice new growth on pine trees and the warmth of the morning sun on your cheeks. You wish you had spent more time with your kids when they were little, and you see their faces in your grandchildren. You *don't* take the same pleasure in landing another contract or buying a bigger car. Nothing is simple anymore. You discover you are no longer content to accept the immediate and move on. Time is precious and you want your efforts to be used where they can do the most good, not wasted on inconsequential things that don't really matter. That's when you know you've reached midlife.

Meaning, vision, personal mission—life takes on greater importance when the distance ahead is shorter than the road behind. We have a natural reluctance to leave without a legacy. A career transition puts a stop to forward momentum and provides time for introspection. Your "life's work" becomes more important than just making a living. My midlife clients are much more likely than their younger counterparts to hesitate when a job offer comes from a company whose products or services do not match their own value systems.

CASE STUDY: Terry R. was the controller for an insurance company. He'd risen through the accounting department to the job of his dreams, but it all ended when a new president came on board who brought along his own financial chief.

Terry did the most aggressive job search of any client I've ever had. He frantically chased every opportunity, determined to get back to work. The first offer was everything he had hoped for: a 20 percent increase in pay, title of chief financial officer, and commensurate perks. He was so excited he stumbled over his words as he told me about it. Finally, he stopped for breath and I asked, "Is their product something you can be proud of?"

A look of surprise came over his face, and he paused before answering. "It's a company that manufactures gaming machines."

Terry is a deeply religious man and the father of two teenagers, so I wasn't surprised when he decided to turn down the offer. For Terry, my question was a wake-up call. He realized at that moment how important it was to integrate his personal values with his professional life. It changed the focus of his search and he began to seek opportunities with companies that contributed to society in ways he thought were important. A short time later he accepted a position with an athletic-wear manufacturer that is recognized as a leader in corporate citizenship.

CASE STUDY: Tom S. was vice-president of international marketing for a company that produced steel pipes. He traveled extensively and pretty consistently missed his daughter's basketball games. As a high-school junior, she was being recruited by the University of New Mexico, yet her father had seen her play no more than four or five times. When he came into my office after he lost his job, the first words out of his mouth were, "I spent 230 days on the road last year. My top priority now is to be home with my family. My daughter will be off to college in two years and I don't even know her. A big salary and an exciting job don't mean much when I'm missing out on being a father."

His unexpected midlife career transition gave him the opportunity to rethink what was important to him. He chose spending time with his family. He was fortunate to have an excellent reputation in the field and to have made many good contacts over the years. He used them to build a consulting practice, making time to attend his daughter's home games. Every now and then he misses the travel and the competitive nature of international sales, but it's worth it.

◙ YOUR MISSION IN LIFE

Complete the following sentences and then write a brief paragraph that expresses your personal mission in life.

1. I believe I was born to _____.

2. I would like to be remembered as _____.

3. The world would be a better place if I _____.

4. I can serve as a role model for _____.

5. If I knew I had only six weeks to live, I would _____.

6. Life has the most meaning for me when _____.

7. Above all, I think it is important to _____.

8. My fondest hope is that _____.

9. The anchor I can always count on is _____.

10. My family would describe me as _____.

◙ PERSONAL LIFE MISSION

_____

_____

_____

_____

_____

■   ■   ■

What Makes You Tick?

Do you make conscious choices or go with the flow? How do you interact with people, deal with challenges, make choices? At midlife, you've established patterns, so there is abundant evidence to help you identify what stimulates you . . . or doesn't. Try to identify which patterns may be handicaps to your success, and which may be precisely *why* you have succeeded. Knowledge is power; self-knowledge is potential. Take time to ponder these questions:

- Are you more likely to be on the giving or receiving end of favors?

- Do you frequently nurture other people or remain somewhat "standoffish?"

- Do you prefer to be alone or to belong to a group?

- Are you a very private person or do you express your feelings freely?

- Do you prefer anonymity or the limelight?

- Are you most often perceived as a leader or a follower?

- Do you question new ideas and new procedures, or are you generally accepting?

- Are you more likely to try something new or stick with the familiar?

- Are you happy just participating or are you driven to win; do you thrive on competition or merely endure it?

- Do you prefer to learn something new or are you more comfortable when you are sure of your skills?

- Are you an initiator or do you wait for someone else to take the lead?

- Do you try to persuade others to believe and act as you want them to?

- Do you consider yourself a risk taker or do you seek stability?

- Is potential or security more important to you?

What do your answers tell you about what stimulates you or compels you to act? These are often called your "personal drivers." Describe the person they reveal.

_____

_____

_____

_____

_____

These questions are the basis for determining what makes you tick, for creating a Personal Profile, developing an Ideal Job Profile, and looking for the Ideal Employer.

What Is the Ideal Job for You?

Use your imagination to create the ideal job for yourself, the job that will optimize your personal characteristics and professional strengths. Describe the responsibilities, product or service, customer base, career opportunities, details of a typical day, culture of the company, and management style.

_____

_____

_____

_____

Who Is the Ideal Employer?

It's decision time. With knowledge comes the responsibility to act. Now that you've spent time considering what is important to you in both your personal and professional life, it's no longer acceptable to say, " I don't know what I want to do." I firmly believe that the answer is within you. The trick is to bring it out of hiding and make a commitment to find your life's work, the work that you do naturally because it reflects who you are.

You have taken a close look at yourself and you have visualized your ideal job. The next task is to develop a profile of the ideal place of work for you. Describe it in as much detail as possible, for if you don't know where you are going, no road will get you there.

- How big is the company?

- Is it entrepreneurial or corporate in nature?

- What is the product or service?

- What is its competitive position / status / future potential?

- What is the company's mission? Its evident values? The corporate image?

- What is the management style?

- What is the communication style? Decision-making style? Employee involvement in strategic direction?

- Is it private or public? Family-owned? Government? Nonprofit?

- Is it committed to social and / or environmental issues?

- Is the company a stable one? Is there growth potential for you?

_____

_____

_____

_____

_____

_____

_____

_____

_____

_____

_____

_____

_____

_____

Your life's work is too important to leave to chance. It deserves your best efforts in the fascinating journey for all your tomorrows. If you have a clear picture of what the destination looks like, you can create a road map to take you there.

CHAPTER FIVE

Powerful Midlife Résumés

*"The way in which we think of ourselves
has everything to do with how our world
sees us."*

—ARLENE RAVEN

YOUR professional history at mid-age is a long one, so it's no simple task to get it all down on paper. Your résumé is the story of your professional life and it should effectively communicate the depth and complexity of your experience. It is also your primary marketing tool, and although it won't land you a job by itself, it can get you an interview for the *right* position. Don't overestimate what a résumé can do, but never, never underestimate it.

Job seekers often encounter a great deal of misinformation about résumés. The reality is:

- Your résumé makes your first pitch to a prospective employer and it deserves your serious attention.

- It is invaluable in positioning you as the lead candidate for a particular position, providing documentation for the interviewer to review later or to pass on to someone else.

- It invariably directs the interview itself, leading the conversation toward the points you most want to discuss.

- Finally, and probably most important, the intense analysis of your background that you will do in order to write your résumé is a valuable self-assessment that will prepare you to tell your story in a compelling way.

The major challenge is presenting your story quickly and accurately at the same time as you stimulate the reader's interest in meeting you. Every word must contribute to the total picture of who you are and what you bring to the table. In an ideal world, your résumé should be so complete, and your capabilities so clear, that you won't even have to discuss your work history in the interview. You'll be able to concentrate on what both you and the potential employer are more interested in—your potential future together. Let's face it, people would much rather hear about what you can do for them right now than about what you did for your past employers.

In most cases, at least five candidates will be interviewed for an opening. They'll all be pretty equally qualified, so it's important to paint a distinct portrait of yourself on paper before you walk in the door. A well-written résumé can create a verbal picture of your personal style as well as your professional capabilities and give you a real advantage by establishing a comfort level with the interviewer before you even arrive. During the interview you'll be free to focus on the future rather than belaboring the past.

Don't even consider hiring someone to write your résumé. You are the only one who knows your story, so the hard work will be up to you. Writing a good résumé is a long, arduous task that can easily take thirty to forty hours of concentrated work. Clients often tell me it's one of the most difficult things they've ever done, but also one of the most worthwhile.

Don't be concerned about the length of your résumé; focus on telling your story effectively. At your age, if all you have to say can be written on a single page, you probably aren't the person they need anyway. As employers become more particular in their hiring, the one-page-résumé rule has fallen by the wayside. They want the whole story. In today's rapidly changing workplace, employers face the difficult task of assessing your potential to handle unforeseeable challenges; gone are the days of simply determining competency. If your résumé is prioritized properly, and the information is helpful to someone in making a hiring decision, it doesn't matter how long it is. On the other hand, if it contains one unnecessary word, it is one word too long. Presentation, readability, clarity, and accuracy are critical.

Does the reader have a complete picture of you and your professional background? Include *all* relevant information concerning your work history, regardless of the job for which you are applying. In a close competition, professional experience *outside* the field can make the difference in getting the position. You never know exactly what a potential employer is seeking (nor do they often realize it themselves), so it is foolish to write a résumé to fit a specific job description. Of course, you may rearrange various accomplishments to highlight a particularly relevant point, but don't cut things out. If the accomplishment was important to you and it represents you effectively, it should be in your résumé. You will be selected for an interview and considered a serious candidate not because you're merely qualified—many applicants are— but for the "added value" you bring. What can you provide that is *more* than they are asking for? Your age is definitely to your advantage, because you have an extensive background someone younger can't hope to match. To include less than you have actually accomplished is to sell yourself short and destroy that advantage.

What is a reasonable résumé length? Most of my clients can write one effectively in two to three pages. However, the types of positions you held and the number of employers may add to the length.

Highlight the Age Advantage

A common midlife misconception about résumé writing is that it should cover only the last ten years of your work experience. Ridiculous! This automatically limits your ability to display the wealth of experience that is your competitive advantage. For example, progressive levels of responsibility over a number of years prove your capabilities and demonstrate the trust former employers have placed in you. As a result, a prospective employer will conclude there is very little risk in hiring you.

Are you looking for a job in a field where major presentations or published papers are important requirements (i.e., academia or consulting)? If so, listing them in an addendum is an effective way of establishing your credentials in comparison to less experienced applicants.

Have you designed products or programs that represent the wide range of your expertise? Don't undersell yourself; give them the whole story. For example, one of my clients is a mechanical engineer who has worked in several industries, including aerospace, high tech, submarines, steel casting, and even food processing. It is this creative and flexible range that gives him an advantage in the job search and he displays it proudly.

Training (professional courses, seminars, and workshops that companies provide for their employees) has become a major business over the last twenty years. It is also a major expense item, so there is increasing interest in hiring in-house "trainers," people who are licensed, certified, or simply very knowledgeable, who can provide workshops to less experienced employees as part of their job. Class topics range from specific technical programs to management strategies, diversity issues, and even how to deal with difficult people. Training is often an excellent opportunity for people at midlife, particularly in smaller companies, which need the expertise but can't afford a full-time training department. If you have had any training experience, including presentations to outside groups, be sure to put this on your résumé.

Today's marketplace demands flexibility, the willingness and the ability to tackle new projects with very little prep time. One advantage to hiring older people is that they have probably worked on something similar in the past. They instinctively know where the trouble spots are and anticipate problems. That's the reality. However, studies done by AARP and other organizations consistently show that hiring managers and human-resource professionals believe older people are inflexible and uncomfortable with anything new, so they avoid hiring them for today's fast-paced, ever-changing work environment. It is critical to prove those misguided perceptions false in your case by pointing to times you volunteered for new projects, designed something innovative, initiated cutting-edge strategies, or simply implemented new policies. If your career has been diverse, it's a real plus. In the past, looking like a "job hopper" was a negative; today it shows your flexibility. Fifteen or twenty years with the same company can be a real handicap unless you break that time down to show how you've grown throughout those years.

There is a natural tendency to believe what we see in writing. You have complete control of how you present yourself to prospective employers on your résumé because, at least initially, your account is all they have. Be aware that unsupported or contradictory claims will land your résumé in the circular file without further consideration. Do not overstate, but remember it is just as dishonest to understate and provide only a portion of the story.

You wouldn't go to an interview sloppily dressed, and there is no excuse for a résumé that is anything other than perfect. Forget computer software templates and programs. In addition to the fact that these formats are typically out-dated, using one immediately positions you as a "generic" product. Chiefly, it shows you haven't paid serious attention to evaluating and communicating your own professional background. It looks like you just don't care enough to do it well. Who wants to hire someone with that approach?

Basic Rules for Résumé Presentation

- A résumé should be printed on high-quality, twenty-four-pound bond paper, in neutral colors (white, ivory, or gray). Whichever color you like best is the right color, a visual reflection of *your* taste, which helps communicate your personal style.

- Fonts can also reflect your personality. Choose them carefully, and be sure you feel comfortable with the way they represent your work identity and who you are.

- Résumés should be free of typos, misspelled words, and bad grammar. Put that word processor to work!

- Send your résumés in eight-and-a-half-by-eleven-inch en-velopes. Folding them into a business envelope makes them difficult to read and hard to reproduce.

- Leave out personalized graphics unless you have a very good reason to include them (i.e., designers and advertis-ing pros can sometimes use these gimmicks effectively to show style and get attention in a field that relies on visual impact).

- Don't include references on your résumé; submit them on a separate sheet.

- Don't include salary information or personal information such as age, marital status, number of children, or hobbies or interests.

Remember, a résumé is you in written form, and anything less than a professional presentation is unacceptable.

Tell It Like It Is

A résumé shouldn't be boring, unless your professional life has been boring, and you certainly don't want to admit that, even if it is true! In order to be credible in the interview, the words you choose to describe your experience on paper should sound like your style of speech. There must be a match between the person on paper and the person sitting in front of the interviewer. One of my clients left a company where he was a business unit manager because he didn't like the culture. The company he left was very autocratic and hierarchical, while he was a strong believer in teams. When he first showed his résumé to me, it was full of phrases like "drove the development . . ." and "personally controlled the day-to-day operations of . . ."—hardly phrases that reflected a "team" approach. When I asked him to tell me about his personal management style, he used phrases like "facilitated a group . . ." and "achieved consensus. . . ." I couldn't help but think, "Will the real manager please stand up?" The contrast between what he had written and what he said was dramatic. He was so used to the jargon of his former company that it had become second nature to talk that way, even though he had left the company specifically because he *didn't* like the management style. Your vocabulary should fit you and your beliefs.

Age: Hide It or Flaunt It?

Let's be realistic. When you walk through the door for an interview, your age will be obvious. It's foolish to try to cover it up on your résumé. Why risk having the interviewer feel you have been deceptive? The whole point of your résumé is to convince the reader of your capabilities, and at midlife you have had more opportunities to develop these capabilities than younger applicants. Flaunt it! Then sell the reader on the idea that your age is an advantage.

We can't ignore the fact, however, that your age may keep you from getting the job. This fact is unrelated to your implied age on your résumé. For the employer who is going to discriminate because of age, attempting to hide it will just delay the process and waste time for both of you. There's a better way. Your age gives you credibility. A good offense is always better than a good defense; so instead of telling only part of your story in an attempt to cover up your age (which in the end won't work anyway), be very up-front about it and let it be known that precisely because you *are* older, you possess the depth and breadth of experience needed to get the job done right.

Résumé Format

There are three basic formats for résumés: **chronological, functional,** and **combined.**

The **chronological** résumé starts with your most recent work experience, and is by far the most popular with hiring managers and recruiters. It's easy to read, logical, and the reviewer is able to absorb the information with little effort.

It's also easy to compare applicants with this type of résumé (not always a point in its favor for you!).

The **chronological** format is the logical choice for the person who has had step-by-step progression in one professional arena. It displays this progression well, and it is very effective in highlighting the extensive experience typical of someone with twenty or more years of experience in one field. For someone who has had several different jobs, however, the chronological résumé can make them look like a "job hopper" without direction.

The **functional** résumé is organized under topical headings of areas of skill or experience. Because it is sometimes confusing to follow, requires more study and evaluation, and is difficult to compare with other résumés, professional recruiters may ask applicants to convert the functional résumé to a chronological format. However, if you have a varied background, it can be useful in categorizing your experience under headings such as marketing, management, budget management, project management. It is also used by applicants who want to obscure an inconsistent employment record, or whose titles and employers were not particularly impressive.

A **functional** résumé can provide a logical grouping of accomplishments that highlights the categories of your expertise. It takes the focus off job titles and can be very effective for someone who has had a varied work history or who wants to change career direction.

CASE STUDY: Dave M. was determined to be a COO (chief operating officer). He was forty-four years old and the most determined client I have ever had. The first day we met, he said, "I *will* be a COO, and I'll do anything it takes to get there. I'm the perfect age, and if I don't make it this time, I might be too old the next time. I refuse to take that chance."

The problem he had in writing his résumé was that Dave's previous job titles had all been in finance (i.e., director of accounting and controller). Somehow, he had to convince a potential employer or a search firm to see him as a COO, although he had never held a management position in operations. We accomplished this with a functional résumé, categorizing his experience under management, customer service and marketing, and finance headings and listing accomplishments within each of these areas. The job titles and former employers went on the second page. In this way, we drew the reader's attention to areas of experience that as a whole qualified him as COO material. Focusing on past titles would have automatically eliminated him from consideration.

Special Note: Occasionally, I have women clients who want to return to the professional world after devoting many years to raising families. They may have little or no relevant work experience, but their volunteer activities are often extensive. For these women, the functional résumé can be used very effectively. Together, we organize their accomplishments in the world of volunteer work into categories specifically relevant to the kind of job they're after, such as: marketing experience, management, volunteer organization, budgeting and finance, public relations, etc.

The **combined** résumé can provide the best of both worlds. It lists your positions in chronological order, but within each, the accomplishments are organized under specific functions. The trouble is that this format tends to be extremely redundant, and can be difficult to hold down to a reasonable length.

The **combined** résumé, like the chronological résumé, lists previous positions in chronological order, but here you organize your accomplishments into categories under each job. I recommend this format when you want the reader to focus on what you have done and not on the job titles themselves.

Sometimes, job titles simply aren't that relevant because they don't accurately reflect your responsibilities and achievements.

> **CASE STUDY:** Jane D. had worked for two advertising firms, neither of which used job titles. Every employee was an "associate." The title was meaningless on her résumé; it told the reviewer absolutely nothing about the job or her skill level. There was nothing to be gained by including it, so instead, we categorized her accomplishments under the headings "marketing and sales," "communications and advertising," "public relations and special events," and "project management."
>
> Although categorizing in this way consumes more space, it pays off by helping the reader quickly identify where you might fit as a potential employee.

The point is that there is no "one size fits all" format for résumés. The format you choose depends on your professional history and what you want to emphasize. There are examples of all three formats at the end of this chapter. Each format has its pluses and minuses, and must be considered in relation to your unique professional history.

The Elements of the Résumé

Job Objective: what every résumé should "do without": Including a job objective on résumés is a thing of the past. Today's employers are more interested in what you can do for *them* in the immediate future than what *you* want. There is no reason to include a job objective. The résumé's purpose is to summarize your work history. It's not a wish list. Use the cover letter to describe the position you're after, and to explain how your background and experience suit you for it.

The Summary Statement: your personal sales pitch: The summary statement is the most important part of your résumé. It is your sales pitch, a succinct statement describing what you can do for a prospective employer. Remember that any claims you make here must be substantiated by a detailed list of accomplishments within the body of the résumé. The summary should paint a distinct picture of who you are as a professional, highlighting your expertise and identifying primary skills, as well as give a sense of your personal style, how you go about your work and what it is like to work with you. It should be succinct: brief, clear, and right to the point. Writing an effective summary statement is a challenge, to say the least, but it can be a very powerful tool for the older applicant who can document real-world experience.

Basic Rules for "Age Advantage" Summary Statements

- Do not begin your summary with "twenty-four years experience in . . ." The number of years you've worked in a particular field is not important in and of itself; it's what you have done in these years that is critical.

- Managers should clearly communicate their style of management, the "how" and "why" of their success. At your age, you should have a defined style that your experience proves works. Show you know what you're doing!

- Focus on three to five major points; don't try to list everything you've ever done. Highlight areas where you have demonstrated expertise.

- Underline major points and use bullets to make the statement quick and easy to read. No long paragraphs!

- Avoid clichéd words: "seasoned" is better applied to meat loaf than people. We assume you're "dependable," "reliable," and "conscientious," and certainly wouldn't expect you to tell us if you weren't! "People skills"and "communication skills" are meaningless terms. Does communication refer to sales, arbitrating, giving orders, public speaking, writing reports, computer software, or managing people? People skills may mean you are very persuasive, congenial, and noncontroversial, or it could mean you are an effective supervisor or negotiator. If terms like "detail-oriented," "big-picture thinker," or "results-oriented" really do reflect your style, try to find a more interesting way to say it, as these terms are so overused that they don't paint a clear picture of your one-of-a-kind professional identity.

- Use power words, but be sure they reflect the way you really speak.

- Be ready to support every claim with specific examples. The summary makes bold claims about your skills, and they will be the first things challenged in the interview, providing your first opportunity to show why your age is an advantage.

- Keep sentences short so that the reader—who's no doubt pressed for time—can quickly absorb the material. Studies show the average résumé receives only twenty seconds of attention, so get your points across quickly.

- Identify your professional level and expertise, but be careful not to describe yourself in a way that limits you.

- Choose terms precisely: "comprehensive experience" and "in-depth experience" are excellent terms to describe the background of an older applicant, but they mean two different things. "Comprehensive" implies a wide range of experience in your field. It means you have perspective that would be valuable in positions where strategic, big-picture thinking is important. You identify problems quickly but probably rely on others to do the hands-on work. "In-depth experience" means you have a number of years of experience in one specific area and are probably an expert in the field, so you would do well in tactical situations, rooting out the problem and doing the hands-on work yourself.

Examples of Effective Summary Statements

Joan R.'s summary statement clearly defines her expertise and the corporate culture where she works most effectively. There is nothing ambiguous about either Joan or her statement.

SUMMARY STATEMENT

Resourceful, articulate **Legal Secretary** with 25 years increasing responsibility in

- Investor Relations
- Human Resources
- Labor Relations
- Labor and Corporate Law

"Thrive on challenges in a dynamic environment."

List very specific categories of expertise in your summary if you have an extensive professional background. Bill was sixty-two years old and a highly respected vice-president of a bank when he decided to make a career transition. He was interested in working on a consulting basis, preferably with one firm, and his résumé beautifully demonstrates specifically what he brings to a new company.

PROFESSIONAL SUMMARY

Extensive experience in **Asset Management, Financial Litigation**, and **Collection.** Special strengths include a thorough knowledge of consumer law; development of policy and procedure; employee training.

Highlights of Qualifications

- Comprehensive experience in consumer-loan/commercial-lease/ real-estate collections as Loan Adjuster, Loss-Recovery Specialist, Collection Manager, and Asset-Control Specialist.
- Skilled in building highly successful collection and loss-recovery teams responsible for up to $200 million in consumer-loan portfolios.
- Thorough knowledge of federal and state laws as they pertain to debt collection, repossession, collateral liquidation, and multi-state lending.

Finding qualified candidates who are cultural matches is a big issue for hiring managers. Finance and information systems people are often perceived as living in their own world, but Harry felt very strongly about his department's role in serving the needs of end users. Putting that philosophy right up front in his summary statement was important. Notice how his management style is highlighted by the words "supporter" and "promoter," which he uses to describe himself.

PROFESSIONAL STATEMENT

Accounting/Finance/IS Manager with 17 years experience in both industry and Big Six public accounting. An integral part of the senior management team who provides the financial guidance and resources necessary to make sound fiscal decisions.

- **Team Leader/Coach** in the budgeting process.
- **Designer/Creator/Implementor** of accounting information systems.
- **Supporter** of the end user's right to determine needs and receive information in an understandable manner.
- **Promoter** of supervisors at all levels taking ownership of creating and implementing budgets.

The term "senior executive" is somewhat ambiguous, as it refers to anyone who has been an officer of a company, including president, CEO (chief executive officer), CFO (chief financial officer), and COO (chief operating officer). More recently, I've seen it applied to people with titles such as CIO (chief information officer) and CMO (chief marketing officer). I recommend that you use these specific titles within the résumé rather than in the summary statement. Here, "senior executive" is more appropriate, because it does not limit you. If you have been the president or CEO of a small company, you may be willing to accept a COO position at a larger company, but if you put the higher-ranking title in your summary statement, a potential employer will assume you are unwilling to step down. In short, you won't be considered for an interview. Use the more general term in your summary statement, until you know what the job offers.

Here is how Joe R. handled this situation.

PROFESSIONAL SUMMARY

Senior Executive with extensive experience starting and growing businesses ranging from $50–$250 million in high technology and light manufacturing. Solid background in finance with proven success developing Pacific Rim markets.

"A decisive leader who recognizes the validity of new ventures, realistically evaluates risk,

commits to the changes necessary to be successful,
and knows when to say no."

The question on every potential employer's mind is, "What can this candidate do for me and my company?" The purpose of your summary statement is to answer that question by clearly stating your expertise, style, and most valuable skills. The reader should be able to determine whether you are a viable candidate for the position on the basis of this short statement alone. Remember, a potential employer will spend no more than a few seconds reviewing your résumé unless you give him a very good reason to read further. Be sure your summary statement positions you as a candidate worth further study. It is the "grabber" that gets the reader's attention, and convinces him to call you in for an interview.

Education and Training

For a person at midlife, it's important to distinguish classes and training you've attended in the last five years from the degrees you earned before your career began. Educational programs, professional seminars, and training you've completed recently demonstrate your interest in learning and personal growth and help overcome an employer's concerns about age. The combination of experience and ongoing education is an unbeatable age advantage.

On the other hand, academic degrees or classwork, professional training, or schooling you finished twenty to thirty years ago may have little current relevance. Of course, your degree was an important part of the foundation for your career success and you should include it, but it's better not to include the vintage, as it will only emphasize that your academic background dates from another era. Advanced degrees and special professional certifications (i.e., Ph.D., Ed.D.,

CPA, PMP, PE, etc.) are important qualifications and should be listed immediately following your name or within the summary statement.

Older job applicants have generally attended a great many training classes, professional seminars, and workshops over the years, and I am often asked if they should be listed on a résumé. The answer depends on how such training is viewed within your profession. Recognize, however, that a potential employer is often asking themselves whether older candidates are not only current in their field, but current in their management style. Lack of academic qualifications and formal training may trip up older applicants, so it's better to include too much rather than risk the perception that you are behind the times. Don't forget to include all those workshops on EEOC, diversity training, sexual harassment, discrimination in the workplace, dealing with difficult people, etc. These may be major concerns for potential employers. Interviewers are reluctant to probe your thinking on these issues in the interview, because they could be risking potential lawsuits. Relieve their minds, and remove this block, by listing these classes in the education and training section of your résumé.

Special Note: The best potential job market for older applicants is *not* in the large corporations, which are more interested in younger applicants on the way up. By far the best market for older applicants is in small-to-medium-sized companies, where the depth and breadth of your background means you can cover a lot of bases. The seminars and workshops you have attended over the years (and the manuals you have tucked away under the bed!) can be a real selling point. Don't be surprised if you're asked to lead a focus group or present a seminar or two of your own.

Military Experience: To Include or Not . . . That Is the Question

If military service has been a significant part of your career, it belongs in the professional experience section of your résumé. However, if you served your country many years ago, and for a relatively short period of time, think twice before you include it.

Let's look at the market view. Age and gender are significant indicators of how the hiring manager will view your military experience, and it's unlikely you'll know either when you submit your résumé. So why take a chance? Wouldn't it be better to bring it up in the interview, if you determine that mentioning it will work in your favor?

Another reason to leave out military experience is the hierarchical nature of the armed forces—an organizational style corporate America is working hard to eliminate. Whether you were an officer or an enlisted person, your ability to work well in a more flattened organization will be called into question and you may not be considered for the position at all.

Hobbies, Interests, Volunteer Service

Hobbies, interests, and volunteer service should be included in your résumé only if they relate to your professional life or exhibit skills that are applicable in your work. In some cases, they can be used to subtly show you are a high-energy person in top physical condition. For example, my husband always puts on his résumé that he received his black belt in karate at age fifty. It says a great deal about his character, as well as his physical condition. Earning the rank took five long years of dedicated effort at the same time as he was holding an extremely demanding job. It's also a great conversation piece! People invariably ask, "You're not going to break my desk, are you?"

If you're thinking about including an interest on your résumé, first consider how it will affect your professional story and whether it will position you favorably. You may run three miles a day (good for you!), but this information is probably more appropriately interjected into an interview discussion. However, if you run marathons, that's a different story. This falls in the same category as the black belt in karate.

Volunteer activities are another matter, and this is an area where older applicants often have a real advantage in setting themselves apart from the competition. Leadership roles, established positions in the community, name recognition, the "public persona" you have established are things few younger candidates can boast. These aren't standard résumé elements but they may well help qualify you for the position you're seeking. If so, they should definitely be included. Also, be sure to include professional associations and leadership positions within them.

Accomplishment Statements: Your A+ Report Card

One of the best parts of writing your résumé is telling your story *your* way. No C-minus stuff here, it's all top-of-the-line material. Looking for a surefire way to boost your self-confidence with one simple project? This is it. Anyone, and I *do* mean anyone, who has reached midlife has significant accomplishments. Younger job seekers often have to convince potential employers that they really can do wonderful things, if only someone will give them the chance. Older applicants don't have to rely on an employer's faith; they have proof of their capabilities. The trick is recalling your accomplishments, identifying their pertinent features, and describing them in such a way that the reader understands their relevance.

Accomplishment statements are the heart of the résumé. You list them after each job in the chronological résumé; in the functional they are listed under each category. You may be tempted to focus on your last position, or the last ten years. Resist that impulse; this is the time for in-depth research on the product you're about to put on the market—you. Besides, you may well unearth a past triumph you had completely forgotten about. Breaking sales records several years in a row (or consistently throughout your career) is compelling stuff. Your past accomplishments also demonstrate that you understand the challenges of positions below the one you've just left behind. For example, someone who started by working on the line in a manufacturing plant and then worked her way up to management is probably going to have a better understanding of employees than someone who enters the field as a manager. You've been there, you know what works and what doesn't. This is the advantage of age and experience. No doubt you will include only a small portion of your accomplishments in your résumé, but others are useful for cover letters and interviews. Take the time to write your accomplishment statements and have them available for various venues within the job search. It's a difficult task, but invariably my clients also look back on writing them as a wonderful experience, a reaffirmation of the value they have brought to companies.

Writing the Accomplishment Statement

Begin by making a list of all your past job titles. Now list the major responsibilities for each position. Go back in time and imagine yourself in that job again. Visualize the people, the sights, the sounds, the daily routines, and the crises. What role did you play? Write a paragraph or two that captures that time in your work life; create a word picture that will take the reader there with you.

With this picture in mind, remember what you did to solve a problem, deal with an emergency, maintain stability in a difficult situation, guide others to success, or handle a responsibility effectively. What talent or skill did you use? What was there about you, and the way you approached the situation, that made it possible for you to do the job well? Tell your story in a few short sentences, and include the results. There will no doubt be several statements for more complex jobs. Don't try to condense too much. Be sure the reader can understand the important details.

How was the organization well served by having you as an employee? How did you make a difference in the lives of other people and/or in the productivity and profitability of the company? Did you receive commendations or awards? Can you document any of the results with dollars, figures, or percentages?

Why are you proud of these experiences? Were you happy there? Do the jobs in which you were most successful have something in common? Was it the company culture? The management style? Did you have a supportive boss, or were you able to work on your own, with full autonomy? Did you grow in those jobs, or were you comfortable because you knew the job well? Answering these questions will help you paint a picture of the "real you" and then help you define the journey ahead.

As you're writing these statements, follow a few simple rules:

- Don't get lost in a tangle of words. Get to the essence. Keep statements under twenty words. If you need to include more detail, create a brief outline (see examples below).

▪ Begin each statement with an action word. Choose words that capture exactly what you mean, that suit your communication style. Example: "initiated" means you came up with the concept. "Developed" implies someone else came up with the idea and asked you to prepare a plan for action. "Implemented" implies someone else had the idea and prepared the plan, and then asked you to put it into action. If you really did all three, say so: "Initiated, developed, and implemented . . ."

▪ Focus on results; don't just list responsibilities.

▪ Be specific: don't just say you managed the operation, give details of exactly what that means.

▪ Underline or use bold type for important points.

▪ Quantify, quantify, quantify: use numbers, percentages, and dollar amounts whenever possible to show the impact your accomplishments had on the organization.

▪ Language should be understandable. Stay away from jargon specific to an industry or company!

It's hard for some people to realize that they have accomplished anything beyond just doing their job. At all levels and in all positions, people get extraordinary things done, or they wouldn't be there. People at mid-age are often particularly uncomfortable talking about themselves because their parents and their culture taught them it was inappropriate to brag. But as a wise man once said, "It isn't bragging if it's the truth." Tell your story, tell the truth, and don't hesitate to take credit for your contributions. This is your sales pitch, your chance to demonstrate to potential employers how good you really are.

Examples of Accomplishment Statements

- Directed the development of a financial plan which increased working capital in a $65 million budget from $0.5 million to $7 million. The investment generated an additional $500,000 annually in treasury income.

- Converted customer-service mailings to a computerized process which **streamlined operations and decreased costs by 20%.**

- Consolidated and restructured two districts, achieving savings of 17% in overhead and 20% in construction equipment, and reducing employees by 10%.

- Trained 300+ employees to meet federal and state OSHA requirements for first-aid/CPR, creating an environment capable of handling on-site medical emergencies.

- **Created an innovative catalog** of retail coupons for new product introduction which reduced customer costs up to 30% while increasing vendor sales.

- Designed and produced a mail-order catalog which increased sales 5% to 10% for four consecutive years.

  • Managed a $165,000 production and distribution budget, completing the project on time and under budget.
  • Effectively selected models to reflect cultural diversity, receiving an award from the National Retail Association as "most effective publication of the year."
  • Developed marketing campaign and worked with distributors to provide sales training to retail outlets.

- Updated corporate headquarters telephone directory weekly for 300 employees. Annually updated company directory for 45 mine sites in 16 states for 1,840 employees, consistently achieving over a 97% accuracy.

Putting It All Together

A good résumé can speak volumes and take you a big step toward landing the right job. It's the hook that entices a prospective employer to bring you in for an interview, documenting your professional contributions over the years. For someone in midlife career transition, it is a valuable way of playing up your age advantage because, quite simply, you have more years of experience, with more accomplishments, than someone younger. Nothing succeeds like success. And your résumé is the written proof.

Writing a résumé is not the beginning of the job search process; it's the summation of the entire self-assessment process. It won't be quick or easy. To do it right will take days, and perhaps even weeks, but when you're done, you will take well-deserved pride in it and your professional history. Would you want anything less?

If you have presented your story well, it will command the attention of the people you most want to work with. The rest don't count. This isn't a popularity contest based on numbers; it's a targeted search for the right job, with the right employer. It only takes one—if it's the right one. In the following pages you will find examples of the three styles of résumé: chronological, functional, and combined. The first two, Bill Johnson and Janet Adler, are chronological. The next two, David Joseph and Peter St. James, are functional résumés. The last, Suzanne Lorrette, is an example of a combination résumé.

Chronological résumé

BILL JOHNSON

P.O. Box 578 • Milwaukie, OR 97000   (503) 555-7077

PROFESSIONAL SUMMARY

Extensive experience in **Asset Management, Financial Litigation,** and **Collection.** Special strengths include a thorough knowledge of consumer law; development of policy and procedure; problem solving and training.

HIGHLIGHTS OF QUALIFICATIONS

- Extensive experience in consumer-loan/commercial-lease/real-estate collections as loan adjuster, loss-recovery specialist, collection supervisor, collection manager, and asset control specialist.
- Skilled in building highly successful collection and loss-recovery teams responsible for a $200 million consumer loan portfolio.
- Proven success in developing and implementing uniform collection policy and procedures manual. Lectured to classes on collection procedure, consumer law, and bankruptcy law.
- Thorough knowledge of federal and state laws as they pertain to debt collection, repossession, collateral liquidation, and financial litigation for multistate lending.
- Demonstrated expertise in the evaluation and liquidation of assets, arbitration, negotiation, and mediation.

PROFESSIONAL EXPERIENCE

BANK OF THE PACIFIC, PORTLAND, OR   1992–2000

Assistant Vice-President, Senior Operations Manager

Handled asset control for the third largest financial institution in the United States.

- Implemented California policy and procedure in Oregon and maintained delinquency below 0.5% on a $120 million loan portfolio.
- Coordinated Resolution Trust Corporation loans totaling more than $80 million, which minimized lawsuits against Bank of the Pacific and Resolution Trust Corporation.

METROPOLITAN LEASING COMPANY, PORTLAND, OR   1990–1992
Vice-President, Asset-Control Specialist
Special assignment: selected to analyze, structure, and implement recovery for $32 million portfolio of charged-off and uncollectible leases.

- Recovered $2 million through effective collection activity, repossession and liquidation of assets, litigation, and negotiated settlements.
- Coordinated asset control efforts with the Resolution Trust.

NATIONAL SAVINGS AND LOAN ASSOC., PORTLAND, OR   1984–1990
Assistant Vice-President, ICL Collections
Developed and managed collection and loss-recovery teams responsible for $210 million consumer loan portfolio.

- Increased productivity by more than 10% through training and by development of a policy and procedures manual which resulted in uniformity of collection activity.
- Brought loans into compliance which reduced losses from 15% to 0.2%. Loss recovery improved from 0% to 26% through more effective collection methods.
- Prepared and closely monitored a $2 million budget, consistently returning a surplus of $600,000 to $41 million through recovery.

ACCEPTANCE CORPORATION, PORTLAND, OR   1983–1984
Collection Manager II
Supervised asset control and customer service with a subsidiary of the largest financial institution in the United States.

- Maintained a delinquency of less than 1% for a multimillion-dollar loan portfolio consisting of mobile homes and autos.

CASCADE NATIONAL BANK	1966–1983
Collection Supervisor II, MEDFORD, OR	1979–1983
Loan Service Specialist, PORTLAND, OR	1966–1978

Managed asset control with the largest financial institution in the state of Oregon.

- Supervised a field collection unit that maintained a delinquency of less than 1.5%.
- Reduced charge-off and increased recovery dollars from sales assets by at least 20%.
- Recovered $150,000 in consumer loan losses during an eleven-month period.

PROFESSIONAL AFFILIATIONS

AMERICAN ARBITRATION ASSOCIATION ARBITRATOR

NATIONAL ASSOCIATION OF CHAPTER 13 TRUSTEES

NORTHWEST FRAUD INVESTIGATORS ASSOCIATION

INTERNATIONAL ASSOCIATION OF CREDIT CARD INVESTIGATORS

INTERNATIONAL POLICE OFFICERS ASSOCIATION

American Institute of Banking: Instructor

Consumer Compliance Law

Performance, Planning, and Review

Excellence in Performance

Chronological résumé

JANET ADLER
5426 W Greenwood Pl. (920) 591-0621
Madison, WI 54661

PROFESSIONAL SUMMARY

Experienced **Executive** and **Sales Management Professional** with strong leadership skills and the proven ability to develop and maintain lasting and profitable business relationships.

EXPERTISE IN:

- SALES AND RELATIONSHIP MANAGEMENT
- FINANCIAL PLANNING AND MANAGEMENT
- AUTOMATION AND BUSINESS

"It is a rare individual who does not want to do well. A leader's job is to set the vision, provide the resources, and establish the conditions for success."

PROFESSIONAL HISTORY

NATIONAL LEASORS INTNL., Madison, WI 1988–2000
A Subsidiary of Riley Barnes Inc., a $500-million-per-year leasing/finance company.

Director, National Sales 1989–2000
Managed a customer base made up of 300–500 independent brokers and leasing companies, an indirect sales force of classic entrepreneurs in an industry typically known for traditional conservatism. Distribution channel for NLI's products and services throughout the U.S., which reached over 16,000 individual businesses per year.

- **Increased sales from $70 million to $500 million** within seven years with continual profit increases.
  - ➤ Successfully transitioned 10-person sales force from a group of hunters focused on targeting new accounts to customer-service-oriented people with the ability to listen and adapt.

- – Provided individual training and support to enhance the staff's abilities to handle complex, changing business-relationship issues.
- ➤ Initiated concept of **multifunctional service teams** to focus on the individual customer's needs and improve turnaround times and contact point problem resolution.
  - – Effectively persuaded operations managers to collaborate in development of team structures, success measurements, and incentive programs.
- ➤ **Concentrated resources on profitable customers** and improved customer service by channeling small, unproductive sources through larger, more productive sources, increasing sales by 30% without increasing staff or overhead.
- ▪ **Served as Project Sponsor** of a two-year, multimillion-dollar update project to make the online system more user-friendly and improve functionality.
  - ➤ Functioned as **general business manager** to facilitate decision making process among IS staff, internal operations, outside consultants, and broker customers; mediated disputes and made final decisions concerning design and ultimate capabilities of the system.
  - ➤ Worked with the Change Management Group, and Arlington Consulting, to modify work flows and procedures.
- ▪ Successfully **directed the implementation** of major change from a "good old boy" network system of pricing and incentives to a quantitative, factual, and profit-oriented matrix. Served as in-house consultant to develop a scoring system which made it possible to reward profitable customers, identify potential problems, and improve performance.

▪ Initiated and conducted a series of yearly national and regional round-table meetings with customers to discuss improvements in products and services, explore competitive market pressures, develop new programs, and share business-building suggestions.

Account Executive, 1988–1989
Grew customer base from 10 to 98 in one year, bringing in $5 million per month and exceeding goals by 50%.

▪ Successfully counseled customers in effective business development, operations and tactical strategies, increasing their potential for success as well as increasing company profits.

WEBRING CREDIT CORPORATION Green Bay, WI   1978–1988
Financial leasing and independent broker consortium.

Western Region Area Manager Minneapolis, MN 1985–1988
Managed a direct sales staff of 7 people covering 22 western states and providing a variety of leasing programs to independent leasing companies as well as equipment vendors and manufacturers.
▪ Exceeded production goals each year by a minimum of 20%.

National Program Manager Minneapolis, MN 1984–1985
▪ Initiated and directed company entry into the "small ticket" leasing segment of the finance industry, adding an additional $75 million in yearly business volume by the second year.
  ➤ Conducted market research into potential size of market, profit potential, competitive environment, niche opportunities, and entry requirements.
▪ Introduced, trained, and provided nationwide support to over 200 sales

and support staff, giving them an expanded product line and enabling the company to increase volume production by 5% the first year.

Area Sales Manager Kansas City, MO 1982–1984

Credit Manager/Analyst Kansas City, MO/Minneapolis, MN 1978–1982

EDUCATION

B.S.: Business Economics; NORTHWEST MISSOURI STATE UNIVERSITY, Maryville, MO

PROFESSIONAL COURSES/TRAINING

RILEY BARNES CORPORATE TRAINING

- ➤ Americans with Disabilities Act
- ➤ Gender Communications
- ➤ Interview Skills

- ➤ Change Management
- ➤ Sexual Harassment
- ➤ Communications Skills

LEARNING INTERNATIONAL

- ➤ Professional Selling Skills
- ➤ Negotiation Skills

- ➤ Strategies for Professional
- ➤ Presentations
- ➤ Account Development Strategies

Functional résumé

David L. Joseph

17 Mountain Road • Minneapolis, MN 97000   (503) 555-1512

EXECUTIVE SUMMARY

Extensive **Customer Service/Marketing/Finance/Management** experience including:

- Full P&L Responsibility
- Marketing Strategies
- Product Development
- Acquisitions
- Facility Start-ups

- Cost Control
- Credit-Line Negotiations
- Cost Accounting
- Systems Conversion

"Effective team builder; a systematic and strategic thinker who can solve complex business issues."

KEY ACHIEVEMENTS

MANAGEMENT

- Increased annual division revenue from $4 million to $15 million and added $1,200,000 (10.8%) in pretax income to the bottom line.
- Increased manufacturing output 280% by improving customer service, delivery times, and order-fill rates.
- Increased division revenues by 20%. Targeted new customers and expanded revenue base for customers outside of parent company requirements.

CUSTOMER SERVICE AND MARKETING

- Improved customer support by developing comprehensive marketing strategies ranging from product literature to consumer samples.

- Managed marketing and customer demographic surveys to determine areas of market penetration for existing and new products.
- Established international sales and accounting efforts in Mexico and newly emerging European Communities.

FINANCE

- Located and purchased manufacturing sites and negotiated equipment purchases over $500,000.
- Saved over $3 million in interest expenses over an eight-year period by obtaining low-cost government funding for the construction of a new manufacturing facility.
- Reduced insurance costs over $400,000 annually by recommending and successfully implementing the conversion of an increasingly expensive health-care program to a self-insured system.
- Reduced operating costs over $500,000 by introducing a consolidated control system.
- Successfully converted a manual system to a fully computerized "state-of-the-art" system for a $100 million company. System became the model for the industry.
- Developed and successfully administered a company-wide Retirement Savings Plan and an Employee Stock Ownership Plan for 400 employees.

PROFESSIONAL HISTORY

GENERAL CORPORATION (NYSE Subsidiary—$70 million)   1983–2000
New York, NY
Senior Vice President: Finance

MASTER COMPANY (AMSE Subsidiary—$100 million)   1977—1983
Philadelphia, PA
Vice-President/Chief Financial Officer

David L. Joseph ▪ Page 3 ▪ (503) 555-1512

FOOD INCORPORATED (NYSE Corporation) Philadelphia, PA 1974—1977

Assistant Controller —Meat Division

Cost Accountant —Baked Goods Division

EDUCATION

Master's in Business Administration

UNIVERSITY OF NORTH CAROLINA, Greensboro, North Carolina

Bachelor of Arts, Economics

HARVARD UNIVERSITY, Cambridge, Massachusetts

PROFESSIONAL ASSOCIATIONS

NATIONAL ASSOCIATION OF ACCOUNTANTS

THE EXECUTIVE COMMITTEE: A national organization for Senior Managers, Presidents, and Chief Executive Officers.

Functional résumé

PETER ST. JAMES

1212 Eastohorn St.   (222) 333-4444
Providence, RI 86000

PROFESSIONAL SUMMARY

Operations and Project Manager who increases on-time delivery and decreases field defects while reducing internal cost per unit by:

- Bringing consistency and an efficient, smooth flow to operations
- Creating employee ownership of customer product awareness
- Developing a communications conduit throughout the operation

PROFESSIONAL EXPERIENCE

Kono Soft Inc.   Providence, RI   1988–2000
Software services company which manufactures diskettes, CD-ROM, and DVD; $250 million annual sales; 500 employees throughout North America.

Light Pole Telecom   Lincoln, NB   1985–1988
Diskette duplication, private labeling, and packaging start-up company. $18 million annual sales; 56 employees.

CAREER ACCOMPLISHMENTS

DIRECTOR OF OPERATIONS   Providence, RI

- Recruited to manage the Providence software services manufacturing facility; 80–300 employees; $20–$36 million annual revenue. Focus on mid-sized accounts under $5.6 million annually, duplicating and packaging diskettes for customers such as Comply, Merkendisk, and Yodelson.

- Moved from loss of $5 million in 1995 to a profit of $1 million in 1996 by fine-tuning the organizational structure.
- Won a $8 million account with Tellinet by selling our site capabilities through a one-year campaign to do all of their software manufacturing.
▪ Managed a facility move from 90,000 sq. ft. to 122,000 sq. ft. while starting the release of the Windows software event: 1,000 pallets and 2,800 raw-material part numbers (a 7-week project from build-out to operation).

PLANT MANAGER   Totterdom, Switzerland
▪ Recruited as the Transition Plant Manager for nine months, transitioning facility from an original equipment manufacturer to a service-oriented business; 50–80 employees; $5 million annual revenue.

PROJECT MANAGEMENT

▪ *Special Project Quality Assurance; Williamston, ID:* Recruited for a two-month project to improve the outgoing quality and adherence to production schedule.
    - Established better methods of handling CDs to avoid poor quality by applying software services quality methods such as count verification, and in-line quality control.
    - Improved material handling methods, giving ownership to shift leads, setting up queue areas, and increasing inventory control.

▪ *Facility Start-up; Ocean, Russia*: Recruited to create a manufacturing operation for Kono which would eventually be the flagship facility in Europe for WordLink. After four months, the facility was servicing a $2 million yearly Merkendisk account duplicating 20,000 disks and shipping 5,000 packages on a daily basis.

- Trained three operators who had no software manufacturing experience in the use of duplication, assembly, equipment, mastering, and manufacturing processes.
- Created raw-material part numbers, warehouse locations, and bill of materials on the manufacturing system to facilitate running the business.
- Introduced Merkendisk as Kono Russia's primary customer, bringing their engineers and technicians in to introduce new product releases.

▪ **Intuit** *Contract; South Bay, CA*: Recruited for a three-month project to manage the production from product introduction to shipping for Comhold, a major $8 million yearly revenue software customer.
- Established a specific "owner" in materials, duplication, and assembly on each of the three shifts which emphasized the importance of adherence to the production schedule.
- Reduced the backlog from 12 to 0 within three months.

PRODUCTION MANAGER   Lincoln, NB
▪ Restructured the duplication and packaging departments which produced up to 5,000 diskettes per day and packaged up to 4,000 per day; 30–80 employees, $10 million in annual revenue.
▪ Turned around a disorganized, dysfunctional department which had gone through five managers within three years and made it an efficient, cost-effective operation.
- Improved on-time delivery from 92.2% to 99.6% within one year.
- Brought outgoing quality level from 60% to 98%.
- Reduced production costs by over 99.9%

MATERIALS MANAGEMENT   Lincoln, NB

▪ Reduced inventory from $320,000 to $200,000 within a four-month period, at the same time revenue was rising 10% a month.
  – Initiated a manual process of material requirements planning which was eventually integrated into the BRTK manufacturing system.

QUALITY ASSURANCE MANAGEMENT   Lincoln, NB

▪ Selected to head a newly formed department in response to requirement from Merkendisk for 100% quality assurance on software services for a new product line.
  – Achieved 100% outgoing quality over a five-year period which resulted in Merkendisk using six other Kono sites and becoming Kono's largest global customer.
▪ Developed the Quality Assurance Checkpoints Program throughout the duplication and packaging processes which was so successful that it was exported to three other sites.
  – Created duplication disk-compare quality checkpoint which verified 10% of the lot against the master diskette.

EDUCATION

B.S. Industrial Engineering, University of Connecticut, Storrs, CT

Combination résumé

Suzanne Laurette

345 WATTERSON CIRCLE • BEAVERTON, OREGON 97123 • (503) 555-2222

SUMMARY

A creative MARKETING AND COMMUNICATIONS PROFESSIONAL with a strong technical background. Strengths include:

- Marketing and Sales
- Communications and Advertising

- Public Relations and Special Events
- Project Management

PROFESSIONAL HISTORY

Bridgeport Electric   Portland, OR   1982–2000

MARKETING AND SALES

- Developed and implemented communication programs for commercial retail sales in three states emphasizing direct marketing; increased sales 17% annually.

COMMUNICATIONS AND ADVERTISING

- Managed a broad range of external creative services while directing the development and implementation of marketing, customer contact, and sales materials for over 100 programs in both residential and commercial markets.

PUBLIC RELATIONS AND SPECIAL EVENTS

- Planned, organized and directed 6–8 major business events annually (multistate conferences, symposiums, annual meetings, receptions, sales seminars) which provided an educational forum for key decision makers, policy leaders, trade allies and customers.

PROJECT MANAGEMENT

- Led special task force which researched and resolved customer satisfaction and quality assurance issues for a base of 10,000 customers within six months.

- Evaluated environmental monitoring programs and recommended changes which reduced monitoring without sacrificing effectiveness or reliability of data; saved $10,000.

Martin Enterprises   Portland, OR   1975–1982

MARKETING AND SALES

- Created an innovative catalog of retail coupons which reduced customer costs 30% while increasing vendor sales.

COMMUNICATIONS AND ADVERTISING

- Designed and implemented a computerized budget reporting system which enhanced measurement of advertising effectiveness and return on investment (ROI).

PUBLIC RELATIONS AND SPECIAL EVENTS

- Prepared and delivered highly successful presentations to national, regional, and local business/professional organizations. Trained staff of five in effective presentation techniques.
- Planned and executed an extensive trade-show program. Conceived and managed the production of innovative feature exhibits for major shows, promoting customer participation and supporting corporate identity.

PROJECT MANAGEMENT

- Successfully redesigned the business-education partnership program which saved $20,000 annually while increasing educational participation.
- Received the Governor's Award for outstanding contribution to business-education partnerships.

EDUCATION

B.S. Business Administration, OREGON STATE UNIVERSITY
Emphasis: Marketing, Management, Communications, and Sales

CHAPTER SIX

Casting the Net

"Man is a knot, a web, a mesh into which relationships are tied."
—ANTOINE DE SAINT-EXUPÉRY

Y OU can't do it alone, nor do you need to. Your whole
life is a series of interactions with other people, those
whose lives you touch and those whose lives touch yours.
You are surrounded with faces and voices and memories. The
midlife career transitioner has the distinct advantage of
having acquired an enormous network over the years that
can be activated to create powerful synergy in the job search.
An effective network is based on trust and mutual support.
The most wonderful part is that it is never-ending, for each
of the people you have known has his or her own network,
in an ever-widening spiral that spans the globe. Latch on and
enjoy the ride.

Networking begins with giving, not receiving, and it is
only effective when it continues in this mode. With every
contact you make, the other person must have confidence
that she will receive more than she gives, even if it is only
the opportunity to increase her own network. Networking is
not isolated. As it is fed, it feeds.

Studies of how people find jobs consistently show that

anywhere from 70 percent to 85 percent come through networking. Only about 10 percent get new positions through ads, another 10 percent or so through various employment agencies. It's still "who you know" that really matters. The logical conclusion must be that anyone who is really serious about reemployment cannot avoid networking.

Midlife career transitioners, however, are often handicapped by cultural messages that continuously play in their heads:

"Never ask for anything."

"Stand on your own two feet. Take care of yourself."

"I've always been successful; I can't admit I've lost my job."

"What will people think? What will they say? Will they lose respect for me?"

Independence, success, winning, power, dealing from strength, giving rather than receiving, never, never needing help: These cultural values are the biggest handicap to midlife career transitions. Overcoming the natural reluctance to reach out to other people is the first step in a successful career search. Activate your lifetime network of friends, acquaintances, and business associates and you will have, indeed, a distinct *age advantage*.

Networking is the proactive approach to a job search. It's taking control of your career, identifying the paths that can lead where you want to go, and bringing together your resources to "make it happen." Everyone you have ever met is a potential networking contact. You can informally talk to friends, relatives, business associates—anyone who knows you, respects you, and might help you make an important contact. You can also take the formal approach, making cold calls to people who can give you information about a particular company or industry. This straightforward approach is surprisingly successful, particularly if you come right to the point, tell them what you are looking for, and make it easy for them to provide information or the phone number of a much-needed contact. Respect their time, show your appreciation, and keep it businesslike. This is no time to be shy, nor is it a time to let modesty keep you from letting people know your capabilities and expertise. Undue modesty is basically dishonest, anyway, for it prevents people from knowing the whole story and making judgments accordingly. Be honest, straightforward, and positive.

The Ten Rules of Networking

1. **Make a vow to give more than you receive.**

2. **Follow through.** When someone gives you a contact, you are obligated to make the call.

3. **Have an agenda.** Know what you want to learn from the meeting or phone call and have specific questions to ask.

4. **Don't waste anyone's time.** Be courteous and considerate but remember this is business, not a social call.

5. **Don't ask for a job.** The purpose is to gather information and build reciprocal relationships.

6. **Do your research.** Do not start by asking them to tell you about themselves, their jobs, or their industries. This is your show; ask intelligent questions by learning as much as possible beforehand.

7. **Listen.** Take notes.

8. Tell your own story succinctly and clearly. Be straightforward about your successes, neither bragging nor being falsely humble.

9. Leave your résumé and business card and ask for suggestions of people you might call for further input. Get exact spellings of names and be sure you get their correct titles.

10. Express your appreciation for their time and don't forget to send a thank-you note or e-mail.

Networking has gotten a bad name these last years as large downsizings put hundreds of people out on the street and career counselors advised everyone to pick up the phone and "smile and dial." Needless to say, anyone with an impressive title was inundated with calls, the vast majority from people who had absolutely no idea why they were calling. It was an all-out attack based on the numbers game: call enough people and eventually you'll find one with a job opening. Neighbors who moved away five years ago, the orthodontist who took care of your teenager's overbite, your brother's friend who works in the same building as the advertising agency you'd like to work for: anyone was fair game. One client told me he had made over two hundred networking calls and actually managed to meet face-to-face with over sixty people before coming to my office. The problem was the people he had called had little or no background in his field, nor did they know anyone who did! Quality, not quantity, is the key to effective networking.

Women tend to find jobs more quickly than men specifically because they are natural networkers. They "share," while men deny. When women lose a job, they pick up the phone and call their friends. When men lose a job, they plan ways to keep their friends from finding out about it. When someone asks a woman how she's doing, she tells them about her concerns and how many rejection letters she has received. A man says, "I'm exploring my options." His friends walk away convinced he doesn't need their help.

The "good old boy" network tends to be primarily a social group.

> **CASE STUDY:** Robert L. was a mid-level manager in a school supply company. He had worked his way up the ladder, from traveling salesman to director of operations for the western United States. In the process, he had met innumerable people and maintained friendships that were thirty years old. He also ran five mornings a week with a group of friends, played golf with a regular foursome, and took long weekend marathon bike trips with another group. He should have had a great network, but eight weeks into the job search he sat in my office looking dejected and told me his friends weren't even returning his calls anymore. Robert had come face-to-face with another typical phenomenon of the career-transition networking process. He hadn't asked any of them for their help, but they nevertheless felt guilty because they couldn't help him, so they avoided him. It is a little like people who don't visit friends in the hospital because they just don't know what to say.

Pretending doesn't work. As long as Robert pretended everything was normal, he was in denial and his friends were uncomfortable. Only when he began to share the details about his job search (i.e. whom he was meeting and what his prospects were), and asked them for their ideas did they relax. In the end, they did have useful suggestions and knew people he could meet. He didn't have to do it alone.

Telephone Techniques

There are few things that strike stark terror in most people as effectively as making a cold call. Yet picking up the phone and dialing is the beginning of a process proven to be successful by thousands and thousands of job seekers. So, why are we all so reluctant to make those calls when we have every reason to believe they are the key to finding a new position? Here's how some clients responded:

"I don't know what to say. I don't want to sound stupid."

"I don't know them or how they might react. They might be offended by my calling."

"I hate to ask people for favors. It makes me feel uncomfortable, like I'm begging."

"I can't think quickly enough on the telephone. I'd rather write a letter so I can figure out exactly what I want to say."

"I can't stand the thought of rejection."

"It just gives me cold chills."

Fear of telephone networking seems to know no boundaries. It always amazes me how little difference there is between the most and least confident clients, extroverts and introverts, salespeople and accountants. They all share a natural reluctance to use the telephone to advance their own career prospects. It seems to me their reactions are based on three basic concerns:

- Fear of not knowing what to say

- Fear of rejection

- Fear of looking foolish

In other words, they are afraid of being placed in a position where they are not in control of their own reactions, of feeling weak and powerless. There is a tool available to help you overcome these fears. It is called "scripting." Think of yourself as an actor going on stage. Write the script, prepare for the probable responses, and practice your role (including intonation).

Reaching out and asking for information or for a few moments of someone's time is so little to ask and most people are very willing to help. The telephone offers you the opportunity to present yourself as a real, live human being, rather than just a name on a piece of paper. Here are some techniques to help you with this approach.

Believe in your product: You are the director of marketing and the product is *you*. You must know the product, know the potential market, and honestly believe in your product. You can't convince anyone else if you don't believe in yourself. This mind-set eliminates concerns about not knowing what to say. You have the facts, the data, and the sales pitch.

Establish rapport: Telephone networking is based on building relationships. Whether you reach a receptionist, an administrative assistant, even a temporary employee filling in for someone else, they can be helpful to you. Don't expect to reach the head honcho with every call. In fact, you may get a warmer reception from someone at a lower level. Convince him of your credibility and he'll pave the way to the decision maker.

Learn and remember names: Ask for the person's name, express your appreciation for their assistance, and sincerely ask their advice in reaching the right person. Remember, they have information you need and they have the access you're looking for. They can screen you in or out.

With every contact you make, you are expanding your sales force. Help them to help you. Listen for opportunities to connect so they will remember you next time you call. Humor is good, if it is appropriate, but it can be deadly if it is not mutual. The problem is that what may be amusing to one person may not be to another. The dead silence that tells you they "didn't get it" can set you back on your heels and make it difficult to restart the conversation. On the other hand, being ready to chuckle, or at least put a smile in your voice, is a great way to put everyone at ease.

Know your objective: Why are you calling? Whom do you want to talk to? What information are you seeking? Prepare a one-minute spiel and remember: *Don't conduct the interview on the phone! Don't discuss salary! Don't ask for a job!* The purpose of your call is to set up an "informational interview." If they ask you to tell them a "little about yourself," make sure it's very little . . . about fifteen seconds' worth is enough!

Anticipate the blocks: And prepare responses for them ahead of time.

When you hear: *"I'm sorry. Ms. Jones is out until next week. Can someone else help you?"*

Say: *"I'd appreciate that. Steve Henneford tells me Ms. Jones is probably the most knowledgeable person in the fiber-wire-connector field, and I was hoping she might have a few minutes to answer three or four questions for me. You see, I've been in the industry for over twenty years, but it is changing so rapidly that I welcome the opportunity to talk to the people who are the most well informed. Whom would you suggest I talk with, or would it be better to call back when she returns?"*

This response accomplishes several things. You have established your credentials, making it clear that you respect her opinion and that you will not take a great deal of her time. Furthermore, you've explained that you and Ms. Jones have a mutual friend who has already screened you. Finally, it's clear from your response that you are willing to accept the receptionist's suggestion of someone else who might give you important advice . . . and who, incidentally, may well get you in to see Ms. Jones later.

When you hear: *"Mr. Frankline does not take calls from people he doesn't know."*

Say: *"I can certainly understand that. I realize how busy he must be. However, this will only take twenty to thirty minutes, and I can arrange my schedule to be available whenever it is best for him. This is concerning the new policy on contract workers that he presented to the Human Resource Association meeting last week, which I found particularly helpful in understanding the current trend toward contingent labor. I've found several articles in my own research that I'd like to share with him as well as ask him some specific follow-up questions. Would you mind checking to see if he would be willing to spend a few minutes with me?"*

Here too, you have established a mutual association, as well as a common interest. You are legitimate, and may well bring Mr. Frankline useful information. You have shown firmness, yet flexibility, and you probably are not going to just go away. Remember that anyone who agrees to give a presentation to an association realizes he may receive calls from participants. If he hopes to be asked back, he can't afford to be rude or ignore a member of the audience. Who knows what future opportunities you may have tucked up your sleeve?

When you hear: *"If you're looking for a job, you need to call human resources."*

Say: *"Oh, I certainly would do that if finding a job was my primary purpose in calling. You see, at this point I'm not at all sure I would be the right person to apply for a position in your company. I'm calling because I was told Mr. Renard's extensive background with ABC Financials makes him the best source to learn about the mission and the corporate history, which are essential to determining if this might be a good fit. I would appreciate his advice and certainly would not expect to take more than a few minutes of his time."*

This response clearly indicates you have a purpose in mind and that it is important to you to determine if you can be an asset to this company before applying. It also shows professionalism; you've done your research and identified the specific person who can give you the advice you need. You're not just throwing out a net and hoping to catch anyone who walks into it. Finally, you have assured the receptionist that you will require only a short amount of time and that you have your questions ready so you won't impose unnecessarily.

When you hear: *"We have no openings. Call back later."*

Say: *"I'm sorry. I must not have made myself clear. I am not calling about a specific job opening. At this point I'm merely researching the industry. Can you suggest someone who might have time for a few questions, if Ms. Henry is not available?"*

Once again, you have shown courtesy, flexibility, and professionalism, and best of all, you have kept the conversation going by identifying a specific request and asking the receptionist's help. There is always a good chance of getting to

Ms. Henry through someone at a lower level in her organization, so if it looks like you aren't going to get past her "guard," make a strategic decision to get in to see someone, regardless of position.

Select your prospects wisely: Does the person you're calling really have any reason to want to talk to you? Are you just on a fishing expedition, or is there something of mutual benefit that this contact can provide? Let's be blunt. What's in it for them?

Be prepared for voice mail: Many people think of this as a lucky break. They sigh with relief and know they can say their piece without worrying about dealing with the responses. However, before you get too excited, remind yourself that this is not to be considered a completed call. The chances of the person calling back are slim, to say the least. Don't take this as rejection, it's just the nature of the beast. Most people simply do not feel a sense of obligation to return voice mail. They expect you to call back if you're serious about the contact. A voice-mail message gives them an opportunity to decide if they want to talk to you or not, and they may have their receptionist screen out future calls from you. Think twice before leaving a voice-mail message. It's better to just call back later.

Consider time of day and day of the week: Think about when you are most likely to be receptive to unsolicited calls. It certainly is not Monday morning. Nor is it likely to be around midday, when you're either getting ready for a luncheon appointment or just coming back from one. In general, decision makers are most receptive early in the day, or late in the afternoon. In fact, your most successful calls are very likely to be just before or right after normal work hours. Friday afternoons may be slim pickings, as even decision makers occasionally leave early for the weekend. However, if they are in their offices, they're likely to be more relaxed and more willing to take your call.

Create a professional environment for your call: Stage setting and costuming can make all the difference. Squelch that temptation to make calls in your running clothes, sprawled out in your easy chair. That just won't cut it. This is a business call. Dress appropriately, watch your posture, have an office setup with notepad and résumé at hand. Be sure the TV and radio are turned off, and family members are aware you are now "at work" and not to be disturbed. It's also a good idea to have a full-length mirror to "talk to." Watch your facial expressions; smile. Whether or not you realize it, it will make a tremendous difference.

Keep records: Take notes. Write down the details of your conversation, including casual comments that you might refer to in later conversations. Be sure to restate any appointment information to be sure it's accurate; you don't want to go to all this trouble and then show up a day late for the appointment!

Show confidence, enthusiasm, energy, and interest: You need to use a little psychology with yourself. Very few people actually feel comfortable making these calls, particularly when they are just beginning the process, but you simply must sound confident and enthused if you expect the listener to respond positively. If there is even the shadow of a doubt in your voice, they will sense it and invariably become "unavailable." Use a tape recorder to check yourself and practice, practice, practice. Work on it until you sound convincing.

Recognize that the other person has different priorities: Your career transition and your perceived need to get information and contacts are normally not on the top of the other person's priority list. Time is a matter of perception. What may seem like the edge of a crisis to you isn't even on the horizon for the other person. It's tough to keep perspective, but essential that you neither be too willing to accept "No" for an answer, nor see it as a personal rejection. Smile and vow to call back in a day or two, and you may be pleasantly surprised at the response. Be careful of negative small talk. Keep your sense of humor.

Reward yourself!: Set up a system of rewards for yourself and never make more than five calls at a time. Make the easy calls first to build your confidence. These are calls to people you know well or the ones friends have set up for you, i.e., the person on the other end of the line is expecting your call. Never make calls when you're feeling sick, depressed, or just plain discouraged. Go for a walk; get some physical exercise and fresh air first. On the other hand, if the very idea of making the call is what's making you depressed, the only cure is to just pick up the phone. You might consider calling a friend to practice, however.

Don't call human resources: These are the gatekeepers of the organization. Many companies are very concerned about liability issues that might arise from showing favoritism to potential job candidates by letting them talk to decision makers outside of the formal process. Besides, HR representatives won't be much help in obtaining the kind of information you want. They're also inundated with calls, so don't expect a very gracious welcome!

The telephone is a tool that can make your networking process quicker and more efficient. It allows you to reach a large number of people in a very short time and to get the information and contacts you need to move forward in your career transition. It is neither more nor less than this. Whether or not it is an object to fear depends entirely upon you. With a firm conviction that you have a product that is worth selling and an obligation to put this information into the right hands, you have nothing to fear. Your success will depend upon your attitude, your sincerity, and the contract you have made with your prospective contacts to give more than you receive.

The Informational Interview

Informational interviewing is one facet of networking. Its purpose is to obtain information about a job, company, or industry. It is generally the result of knowing someone, who knows someone, who is willing to get you in to meet with a person who has knowledge or contacts that will get you closer and closer to your real goal—a job. In a large percentage of the cases, however, the information you receive is even more important; it may even make you realize you don't want to be part of this job, company, or industry and keep you from making a serious mistake later.

Informational interviewing is an *age advantage* for the midlife career transitioner. You have the credibility to get in to see almost anyone. Your age alone often opens the door because the prospective contact assumes you will bring something of value to the conversation, perhaps even potential customers or vendors, insight into the market or management techniques, or networking contacts they can use. You just have to knock on the door.

Networking is a process, not an event. It takes time, quite often a significant amount of time, because you must guide the process as it unfolds. It's a little like playing chess, setting up each play with a larger strategy in mind. Informational interviewing puts each play into action and sets the stage for the next. Networking is often compared with pyramid sales because each contact you make should lead you to at least two more. Once again, too many people focus on the quantity of contacts they make without planning the strategy and ensuring that each contact brings them one step closer to the goal. Before they realize it, all their time is taken up by meetings with people who have little prospect of leading them forward. They've lost control of the game.

Questions for the Informational Interview

Industry:

1. Where do you see this industry going in the next five years? Ten?

2. How is it evolving worldwide? Global market potential?

3. What is the competition? Who are the major players?

4. What trends do you see evolving?

5. What types of products do you anticipate becoming obsolete?

6. What factors affect sales?

Company:

1. How would you describe this company's place in the industry?

2. Could you tell me a little about the company's history? How it began? Major changes in philosophy or direction?

3. What is the current market thrust? Strategic direction? Major challenges? Is the goal to maintain market share, move into other markets, increase in size substantially?

4. How would you define the company culture? Is it more entrepreneurial or corporate? What would you say are the core values?

5. What is the management style? Decision-making style? Communication style?

6. Has the company experienced any major changes in the last years? Is it changing now? How does the employee body generally respond to change?

7. What does it take to succeed here?

Job:

1. What are the major job functions? Critical competencies needed? Percentage of time spent in each function?

2. What do you see as the major challenges in the next six months?

3. What are the departments and who are the people this position interacts with the most? Who are its customers? Its biggest support system?

4. What characteristics are the most essential to succeed in this position?

5. Is this job based more on maintaining an already successful program, providing innovation and change, turning around an organization in trouble, establishing new priorities and goals, building a team, or empowering people to do what they already do well?

6. What flexibility would I have to make changes? What resources? What support would I get from other departments as well as senior decision makers?

7. How would you describe your management style? How do you like to have people communicate with you? Memos? Staff meetings? Face-to-face discussions?

Informational interviewing is the research process that ensures an effective career transition because it gives you the opportunity to gain insight, acquire useful information, and make contacts that will not only make the job search easier and more productive but will ensure a support team to make you more successful once you start the job.

Networking As a Lifestyle

Conducting a job search without networking is like swinging on a trapeze without a safety net. It might work, but then again, it might not. Why take the chance? Even more important, however, networking with integrity is a life skill that will enrich every element of your life.

Networking is the greatest usage of your energies because it is an activity that never ends once it is begun. It is a self-perpetuating, ever-growing, and continuously evolving process whose lifeblood is trust and faith in the inherent goodwill of other people. How can it fail?

CHAPTER SEVEN

The Art of Interviewing at Midlife

"Fortune favors the audacious."
—ERASMUS

"TELL me about yourself."

Seven anonymous faces stare impassively at you, and a shudder runs through your body. All you want is to be somewhere else, anywhere else, and you wonder, once again, how you came to be in this situation. Seated at the head of the conference table, in a stark, impersonal room, you look at each of the people in front of you and realize they are no more eager than you are to spend the next hour in this carefully structured interview (devoid of opportunities to relate in meaningful ways). It's a scene from *Brave New World*, a mechanized ritual many organizations believe will select the "right" person for the job, precisely because it has been purged of subjectivity. Welcome to the Panel Interview.

The hardest part of the job search process, particularly for someone at midlife, is going through the interviews. You're put on the defensive, stripped of identity, and exposed to the indignity of strangers judging whether or not you are capable of handling a job you've successfully performed for years. It's hard to believe that just a short time ago you were on the other side of the desk, with power to hire or fire, promote or ignore. The first interview generally comes before you have really processed your own job loss, much less regained the energy and enthusiasm you'll need to make a good impression. Still, you've gone through a self-assessment process; you know your product, you've rehearsed your two-minute spiel, and you think you're ready to face the music . . . until you see the bored faces across the table. Suddenly your confidence and enthusiasm disappear, and you ask yourself, "What am I *doing* here?"

The cold realization begins to surface: You are on your own in front of strangers who are there to judge your professional worth. You're a jumble of emotions: anger, resentment, fear, loneliness, indignation, panic, and finally, resignation. If you have recently lost your job, you can expect to be angry, hurt, resentful, frustrated, and just plain depressed. In most instances, your feelings will be written all over your face. Stay away from interviews until you have your act together and you are able to come in looking and feeling like a winner. This also holds true for those informational interviews and networking interviews your friends want to set up for you. Interviewing too early in the transition process is a big mistake, simply because you'll be wearing your pain on your sleeve. Don't take a chance on losing a good potential opportunity by blowing the initial contact; save it until you're ready to knock their socks off.

Few midlife career transitioners are prepared for the interview process. A large percentage have never been interviewed, obtaining their first jobs through informal networking, and then either moving within the same company or being recruited to other companies. Although they have participated in interviews throughout the years, they have not had to face the process themselves. For many, the experience is demeaning and demoralizing. However, like any new experience, practice helps and, in time, most people learn to deal with the various interview formats, and even develop a degree of objectivity that makes the ordeal less personally invasive.

Think of it like this: An interview is a precontracting meeting between two professional peers. The interviewee is an equal partner in the process, and should not allow himself to feel like a victim, or to be treated as anything less than a professional peer. Do everything in your power to keep the discussion focused on business. Make a conscious effort not to let it negatively affect your perceptions of personal worth. It will help if you consider yourself a "consultant," with the background and expertise to counsel the potential employer, and their representatives (interviewers), on the position requirements and how you can assist the organization in achieving its goals. It is not a matter of "being chosen"; it is a matter of mutually determining if the company and the job fit your background and goals.

Preparing for the Interview

People hire winners. The older job seeker has the advantage of having made numerous presentations over the years. She's been in the hot seat, defending positions and persuading coworkers and managers to accept her ideas. She's had to sell herself and her ideas, over and over again. Interviews aren't much different. They are simply marketing a product, so follow all the rules for good marketing: analyze your product, know its strengths and weaknesses, know the market and the needs of the buyer and how your product can fulfill those needs, and then present it to its best advantage. Neither undersell nor oversell, because the goal is to find the perfect fit where your product will be most successful.

Is your interview outfit helping or hindering your professional image? Are you sure it isn't "circa 1970"? Your best friends (and family) are often reluctant to tell you you're out-of-date; they don't want to hurt your feelings, and besides, they're used to seeing you like this. Hie thee to a store that deals in upscale professional attire and seek the advice of a personal shopper. Most of the better stores provide this service at no cost. This is called "Investment Dressing" and it well may be the best investment you'll ever make. You've got to look the part if you expect to be hired for an important position. After all, you are also an important investment for the company. You may have a strong sense of your personal style, but for now, take the advice of an image consultant over that of a spouse or best friend. Choosing the right image consultant is like choosing a consultant in any other field. They need to get to know you: your personality, your profession, your communication style, and the image you want to project. Count on the initial consultation taking at least an hour; after that time the consultant will make selections and recommendations for you to consider. When you look good, you feel good, ready to conquer the world (or at least the interview). Note: the high-tech industry has dramatically changed the look of corporate America, where "cool" and "laid-back" are the right look rather than "proper" or even "stuffy." If you don't want to stand out like a sore thumb, lose the pinstripes. It's not necessary to go directly to rumpled blue jeans and tennis shoes, but you should look like you could do so comfortably at a moment's notice. Nothing says you're from a different generation quicker than being too formally dressed.

Do your homework. All the interviewer knows about you is what you tell them, through your résumé, your references, and your own credibility in the interview. You won't be there if they don't already think you can do the job. Few job seekers at midlife realize, however, that they need to research the company and know everything they can about the potential employer. This is something younger people are more likely to do, and it can give them the advantage because they come to the interview informed. Remember, the most fascinating conversationalist is the one who encourages others to talk about themselves. By doing your homework and knowing everything possible about the interviewer and the company, you can position yourself as knowledgeable and interested.

Think of yourself as the host rather than the guest. Most often you will be interviewed by people who do not interview others as a profession, and they are likely to be as uncomfortable as you are. Put them at ease. This may sound like a reversal of roles, but it's just a matter of courtesy. Interviewers who end up hiring an older applicant often comment on how much they enjoyed the interview. I am convinced it's because the person at midlife is generally more accomplished at being a "host" and making other people comfortable.

Learn to understand your own communication style and to recognize the communication styles of others. Carl Jung, the Austrian psychologist of the last century, believed people fit into specific personality types. His work has been a major influence in the communication field, and through the years, various tests and assessments based on his original concepts have been developed to help people analyze their own styles and learn to communicate more effectively. People really do think differently, and they gather the information they need to make decisions in diverse manners. Because the interview is so crucial, anyone entering the job search process should take time to analyze how he comes across to other people, and become proficient in reading the styles of others. There are numerous tests and books available, and any good career counselor will be able to provide assessment materials. The following is a relatively simple method that can be very helpful in an interview situation.

Communication Styles

Communication is sometimes a very risky business. Often we believe we're expressing ourselves clearly only to learn that the other person was distracted either by our tone or our body language. In fact, numerous studies have concluded that only 13 percent of our communication is what we say. How we say it accounts for the rest.

An important part of communication is understanding the primary method the other person uses to gather information. What do they need to make decisions, to operate in their world? How do you identify their style and then provide them with the input to influence their decisions? Studies show that the first twenty-five seconds of the interview often determine if you will be hired. You have only one chance to make a good first impression. Whether or not you really have only twenty-five seconds to do so, there is no question that the initial impression sets the mood for the rest of the meeting. Pacing, and "getting on the train" with the other person, is largely up to you.

The ability to recognize a communication style and smoothly adapt your own to match the other person's is a skill that can be learned. Dr. Carl Jung identified general characteristics of the four major styles, which I've renamed: the Action Person, the Data Person, the Idea Person, and the

People Person. Everyone uses each of the four styles at various times, in various situations, in varying degrees, so each of us is able to adapt to someone else at least for short periods of time, enough to get through an interview at least! A small percentage of people among all four styles—no one approach dominates. With them, it won't really matter how you communicate, because they'll fall into step with you. It's the people who have very dominant styles that will require your flexibility and sensitivity.

Understanding communication styles can give you important clues about whether or not you and the interviewer would work well together. Some people change styles dramatically in crisis situations, while others remain relatively consistent. Obviously, these people are generally easier to live and work with, simply because they are more predictable; we know what to expect from them. During interview situations, neither interviewer nor interviewee is likely to be in her comfort zone; therefore, it is important not to jump to conclusions about what it might be like to work with this person.

The basic overview of the four styles that follows includes special reference to interview situations.

The Action Person:

Favorite phrases: "Take charge." "Make it happen." "Just do it!" "If we make a mistake, we'll try something else." "Results are what count!"

Communication style: Abrupt, direct, forceful.

Time focus: Now!

Greatest strengths: Ability to make quick decisions. Strong sense of responsibility. Cram twenty-six hours into every twenty-four-hour day.

Greatest weaknesses: May make decisions without thinking through the consequences (however, this may only be the perception of those people who are less comfortable making quick decisions). Often perceived as domineering, bossy, aggressive—the result of an overly developed sense of responsibility and a determination to get things done. Sometimes insensitive to other people.

Typical dress: Haphazard. They are moving too fast to care much about how they look. Men are likely to have their sleeves rolled up, ties askew; both men and women are likely to have jackets thrown over a handy chair.

Movements: Quick, determined, strong.

Desks: Piled with papers, yesterday's sandwich crumbs, coffee spills. Interestingly enough, they can usually find anything they want very quickly.

Interview style: Brusque. Remember, they are responsible for the world. They don't believe it can function without them for an hour, so expect constant interruptions: phone calls, people coming in to get signatures or ask questions. The Action Person has a short attention span and isn't interested in your belaboring your past accomplishments. Emphasize your own ability to take charge and get things done. That's all they want to know. Save the details and specifics for the Data Person.

The Data Person:

Favorite phrases: "Do it right the first time, and we won't have to do it over." "I'd like to see the data on that." "The facts show . . ." "I never let emotion influence my decisions."

Communication style: Slow, pedantic, measured, precise.

Time focus: The past, where the facts and data can be collected.

Greatest strengths: Precision, accuracy, predictability. They make very few errors, can be relied upon for accuracy, and will not be swayed from firm convictions.

Greatest weaknesses: Unable to make a decision (because it is usually impossible to have all the facts and data). May be very inflexible and unwilling to try something new, therefore may miss opportunities.

Typical dress: Usually immaculate, perfectly groomed, rather formally attired.

Movements: Measured, may appear to hang back rather than step forward, to wait and observe before committing to action.

Desks: CLEAN! The Data Person will generally have only the work they are doing at the time on their desk; in this case, your résumé and a notepad. They are great note takers, as they are always "gathering data." Another clue to their communication style is awards, certificates, diplomas, or engraved pen sets, which testify to past achievements.

Interview style: Formal. The Data Person does things properly, and they will regard this as a business meeting that requires proper decorum and ritual. No chitchat, please, other than initial pleasantries. They will want facts, data, precise information about your past accomplishments. The more numbers and proof you can provide, the better. Letters of reference are welcome . . . more data. Remember, Data People are not risk takers. They want to be absolutely sure before they make a decision, so the more specific information you can give them, the more likely they will be to feel comfortable hiring you. Above all, don't frighten them by implying you make decisions easily or quickly. They want to know you will analyze and review the "data" with a number of people before you take action.

The Idea Person:

Favorite phrases: "On the cutting edge . . ." "Conceptually, . . ." "Where do you see this going in the future?" "Leading the competition." "What if . . . ?" "How does this tie in with our mission?"

Communication style: Fragmented, bouncing from idea to idea, enthusiastic, difficult to follow.

Time focus: Future.

Greatest strengths: Creativity, ingenuity, flexibility, innovativeness, idealism.

Greatest weaknesses: Impractical, poor implementers, may jump from idea to idea without ever landing or getting anything done. May spend their time brainstorming, with little focus or direction.

Typical dress: Either "avant-garde," stylish, and "far out," *or* the "absentminded professor" caricature: rumpled with no recognizable style. Socks may be unmatched, nothing really goes together.

Movement: May be either vague or agitated. Typically poor eye contact, gazing upward (seeking a vision?). Relate better to ideas than to people.

Desks: Eclectic. These are fun people to buy gifts for, as they love gadgets, puzzles, and strange things that float on oil or defy the laws of gravity. Reading materials will be heavy-weight, often related to their profession, but may also reflect other interests.

Interview style: Also eclectic. Remember, ideas are their thing, not people. Your value will be reflected in your ability to spark these ideas. They have little or no interest in your past accomplishments. Yesterday is over; today is a necessary evil; tomorrow is what really matters. You will have to keep them on track. Your best chance of being hired is if they see you as sharing their "vision."

The People Person:

Favorite phrases: "We're a real family here." "I feel . . ." "Our employees are our greatest assets."

Communication style: Warm, friendly, sometimes overly personal.

Time focus: Past and present. Relationship-oriented; nostalgic.

Greatest strengths: Genuinely like people. Caring, sharing, nurturing. Value people as individuals and as teams. Appreciative, considerate, sensitive, intuitive.

Greatest weaknesses: May weaken other people by being overprotective or sympathetic. May be perceived as intrusive or overly familiar. May be considered weak leaders, easily distracted by "people issues." May have their feelings hurt very easily or absorb other people's pain.

Typical dress: Comfortable. Soft fabrics, often with pleasing textures. Prefer pastels or soft prints. Men often wear cardigan sweaters and may wear ties with scenes or children's drawings. Women often wear knits and scarves.

Movement: Welcoming, enfolding, touching, nonthreatening. Hugs and two-handed handshakes are a sure sign you are in the presence of a People Person.

Desks: Full of motivational plaques and family pictures, small mementos.

Interview style: Conversational. Although you will no doubt enjoy this interview style the most, you will be the least likely to know how you have done. The People Person likes everyone! Unfortunately, they can't hire everybody. Regardless, everyone leaves feeling sure they are the chosen one. The real challenge here will be to keep the conversation somewhat directed toward the job. This communication style is more likely to focus on your family and theirs, the company picnic, and long stories about employees who have been at the company over thirty years. A nice place to work, but a tough interview to really show your stuff. The bottom line, however, is they don't hire anyone they don't think is "nice," so remember everything your mother taught you about finding something good to say about everyone.

Understanding communication styles is as critical to making a good impression as it is to doing your job effectively once you are hired. Which style is most typical of you? What can you do to make yourself more comfortable with styles quite different from your own? It isn't a matter of being someone different than you are; it's just a matter of sensitivity and realizing that people do not all communicate in the same way, and they certainly make decisions based on different criteria. Being forewarned about the styles can help you make the interviewer comfortable and make it easier for you to present your case.

People of mid-age are often more uncomfortable in an interview situation than younger people. This is partly because a large percentage of them have never interviewed for a job, or at least for many years, but a major factor is that it can be embarrassing, even demeaning, to be asking for a job at this time of life. It's tough on the ego. The key is to realize that you are an equal partner in this important "precontracting" meeting, and that you must be proactive in ensuring that honest, comfortable communication takes place. At midlife, you've worked with all types of people in a variety of situations, some more difficult than others. You may have given little thought to styles of communication. You've simply dealt with different people in different ways, quite naturally. My experience, however, is that understanding your own style and learning to quickly identify the styles of others can be the difference in whether or not you are hired. You're on unfamiliar ground in an interview, and the person on the other side of the desk won't always recognize your value; it's up to you to be sure real communication takes place. Matching communication styles and making them work for you can be a major *age advantage*.

Interview Formats

The interview process has become more and more convoluted these last years, often taking several weeks to complete. It is unusual to be interviewed only by the person who will be your boss; it's much more common to have a series of interviews. Companies have become increasingly wary of making hiring decisions, fearing potential lawsuits if they hire the wrong person and then want to get rid of him later. As a result, they have increased the number of interviews, regimented the process in an attempt to make it completely objective (an unrealistic goal), and have taken numerous precautions in advertising the position and extending the length of time between announcement and hiring in attempts to avoid errors. In many cases, it has become an onerous burden both to the applicant and to the company, requiring an excessive amount of time and stress for all parties. Nevertheless, the interview process is integral to getting a job, and the successful applicant must learn to deal with it effectively. When you are called for an interview, remember to ask these questions:

"What will be the format of the interview?"

"How long will the interview be?"

"Who will be the interviewers? Names? Titles? Departments?"

This information can be vital to your success.

There are six basic interview formats. Understanding them not only gives the applicant a distinct advantage in knowing how to prepare but also provides clues to the dominant communication and decision-making style of the company. This insight can help you determine whether working there will be a good cultural fit; it may even result in your declining the interview opportunity, rather than wasting their time or yours. On the other hand, if you recognize a good potential, this information can be helpful in making a favorable impression, allowing you to effectively match your communication style with the interviewer.

The styles include:

- The One-on-One
- The One-on-Two

- The One-on-Three
- The Panel
- The Marathon
- The Beauty Parade

The One-on-One Interview is typically the choice of the *Action Person* interviewer, a person who makes decisions quickly and easily, who does not require input from anyone else. It is usually considered the easiest interview, because the applicant is interviewed by the person who will be their direct supervisor, and it's typically a clear, focused discussion of the details of the job. The goal is to evaluate whether the applicant has the required skills, and whether she and the interviewer-supervisor can work together effectively. The time between interview and offer is usually short, often just a few days. This is a good interview for those of you who are older, as it places you in a professional peer position, and this communication style encourages you to speak right up and show what you can do, without fear of intimidating the interviewer. The interviewer will be likely to have confidence in you immediately if you show confidence in yourself. Don't hold back!

Strategy: Show you are a take-charge person. "Action" and "results" are what this interviewer is seeking. In other interview formats, this may be considered overwhelming or overly confident, even intimidating, but in the One-on-One, you should show energy and confidence. Shake hands immediately. When the interview begins, sit forward and get to the point. Don't belabor the details or give long explanations, and don't go off on brainstorming tangents. The Action Person is interested in right now, not the future or the past. Attention span may be quite short, so keep your sentences brief and focused. Interview attire shouldn't be too formal; strong colors and comfortable clothing that allows you to move easily and freely are most appropriate.

The One-on-Two Interview comes in two styles. Scenario 1 reflects the *Data Person* communication style. It typically includes the prospective boss and a representative of the human-resources department, who is there to ensure that the interview is conducted by the book. In Scenario 2 you will be interviewed by the person who will be your boss, as well as that person's boss. This is an entirely different situation, one that should throw up red flags because it may well be a signal that the senior person is a strong *Action Person* who has no faith in his subordinate, and may micromanage, making it an almost impossible work environment. These two scenarios are very different and you will need to know which you are facing before you arrive.

STRATEGIES: SCENARIO 1: Whenever the human-resource representative is included, you can expect the interview to be conducted in a somewhat formal manner. You should be prepared for a series of predetermined questions, with little opportunity to explore further areas, because the goal is to ensure that each applicant is given equal treatment. Allow the interviewer to take control: respond directly to each question and refer to numbers and statistics frequently, the "data" this person requires to make a decision. Be serious and attentive, keeping chitchat to a minimum. Avoid loud tones of voice, frequent laughter, or strong arm movements. Interview attire should be restrained, professional, "proper."

SCENARIO 2: You may feel a little overwhelmed by this duo; your best approach is to attempt to include your potential boss throughout the discussion, although the questions will probably be posed by that person's boss. Respond directly. Be careful of getting into an adversarial position, which may happen suddenly if either of the interviewers feels threatened by your age and experience. Your approach, if you really want to work here, is to position yourself as supportive, and ready to take a backseat. Let them know you'll work to make them (particularly the senior person) more successful. As an older applicant, be aware that you might be perceived as someone with ambitions to take over your prospective supervisor's job—not a comfortable position for either of you. Interview attire should be understated, but professional; no "power suits."

The One-on-Three Interview: Once again, this interview format comes in two scenarios. In Scenario 1, you will be interviewed by three people, including your potential boss and two of his/her peers. The interview will be a sound, professional exchange of information, a format often preferred by older applicants. You will typically be treated with respect and courtesy, the assumption being that you have something concrete to offer, and that you are all there to explore the options. This format most closely represents the ideal "precontracting meeting," most often with a less structured and formal *Data Person* communication style.

Scenario 2 is quite another story. This is a favorite interview format of the *People Person,* whose main goal is to ensure that everyone likes each other. Remember, their motto is "We're a family here." You will typically be interviewed by your prospective boss and two prospective peers—another red flag. Unfortunately, this attempt to be congenial and inclusive is almost guaranteed to select the least impressive candidate, because your two potential peers are certainly not going to hire anyone who could be a threat to their future advancement. This is a deadly situation for an older applicant, who often has impressive qualifications.

STRATEGIES: SCENARIO 1: This will be an easy, and often very enjoyable, interview for the person of mid-age. It's just another business meeting, with an agenda, goals and objectives, and mutual respect. Of course, you will want to be sure to show the same regard for your interviewers. Don't try to impress them; treat them like professional equals. Be sincere, collegial, and appropriately serious; they are here because they believe the selection is important to their own responsibilities; this isn't a casual occasion. Interview attire should be appropriate to this level of business meeting; it's better to err on the side of formality.

SCENARIO 2: Understate, understate, understate. Remember, these people don't want anyone who might upstage them. When answering questions, it's a good idea to refer to their expertise and experience and show you will defer to their judgments, or at least consult with them before making major decisions. Are you really sure you want to work here? It's a very difficult situation for an older applicant, because even if you get the job, you'll always have to be careful about intimidating your coworkers. You may waste a lot of time "playing humble." Interview attire should be nonthreatening, i.e., tweedy and understated.

The Panel Interview: This is no doubt the most common, and most hated, of all interviews. You will be interviewed by five to seven people, usually of various levels, selected to provide broad representation of departments within the company. In a somewhat naive attempt to bring total objectivity to what is inherently a subjective process, companies have depersonalized interviewing to the point where you may feel like a victim, being interrogated and judged by people who most often wish they were anywhere else. It's a very adversarial interview, particularly difficult for the older person, robbing them of dignity and professional respect, and often raising negative feelings of discomfort, resentment, embarrassment, and anger. It is the consummate *Data Person* interview, designed to quantify the qualifications of applicants. They may even use some type of matrix evaluation system to score the applicants. The interview is formal, taking place in a conference room, within very specific time limits. The goal is to provide precise structure that ensures equal treatment of each applicant and prevents anyone from having an advantage. The applicant will typically be seated at the head of the table, facing the interviewers. Questions will be predetermined, general in nature; follow-up questions, in most cases, will not be permitted.

Strategies: Be serious, formal, precise, professional, but not intimidating. Think of a court trial and determine how you can be a good, credible "witness." Be prepared psychologically (a major reason why you should always ask about the interview format in advance) so you will be able to handle the situation without becoming defensive or feeling victimized.

Be calm, rational, and quietly in control. One of the difficulties of this format is that the interviewers may come from all areas of the company, and may have little knowledge of your area of expertise. They are also likely to have been selected for this duty and had no choice in the matter. They may visibly show their resentment at being here. Remember, these people are very cautious, and they will want data in order to make decisions. They will usually be asked to give you a numerical evaluation for each of your answers; therefore, it is critical for you to answer every question as precisely as possible. Give dates, figures, percentages, dollar amounts.

This panel is unlikely to hire anyone who makes decisions too quickly, who appears "wishy-washy," or who is prone to create change. They are not risk takers, so innovative ideas are not something they value highly. They are much happier with analysis and research based on past statistics rather than projections for the future. Interview attire should be of the navy blue suit variety, for both men and women; professional, immaculate grooming is required. Watch those shoes! Be sure they are polished (no run-down heels, please). This is certainly an interview the older applicant can handle well, especially if they also fit the Data Person mold. The critical point here is to know what you are facing, to understand the format and the communication style it represents and not to be intimidated or insulted. Whether or not this interview process selects the most qualified person is questionable at best, but it has certainly been popular these last years with companies who want to believe it's possible to select the best candidate without engaging people in honest dialogue.

The Marathon Interview: In my opinion, this interview format is the most apt to select the person who will be highly successful in the position, and it is the interview where people of mid-age really shine. It involves a series of interviews over one, two, or even three days. You may meet with your prospective employer for an hour or two, with individuals and groups from other departments, with your own prospective work group, and with various others. It is exhausting, invigorating, interesting, and a bit overwhelming all at the same time. It demonstrates the company's solid sense of professional respect as people of goodwill genuinely share information and ideas. Older applicants typically handle meeting with a variety of people and interests well, and feel very comfortable in the role of welcome guest. Their breadth and depth of background make it possible for them to interact and appear knowledgeable in many areas of the organization, and precisely because of their age, they come to each encounter with instant credibility. They are expected to do well, and they do. An added bonus of the Marathon Interview is that it establishes the foundation for a good working relationship once you are on the job. You have already met the major players and they have bought into your success.

Strategies: Be yourself. Be gracious. Don't try to impress, just participate openly and evenly in the discussions. Be physically "up" for the occasion, because it really can be exhausting and you don't want anyone worried that you lack the energy required to take on the job. Disabuse them of this notion by preparing for the interview as you might a real marathon: exercise, get a good night's sleep, eat a good breakfast, wear comfortable shoes, and be "rarin' " to go. Note: it never hurts to carry a "Power Bar" or two, either. These interviews are famous for running behind schedule and leaving no time for lunch or a break.

The series of interviews moves so quickly that you will soon realize you have no idea what you have said to anyone. Take notes, if you like, but if you repeat yourself, it probably won't matter. Face each encounter with optimism and enthusiasm, and all will be well. Interview attire should be professionally appropriate to the position, and very approachable. This is a company that knows how to treat people, and you'll enjoy being there. As for communication style, this format reflects a nice combination of all four, and you'll be interviewed by people of all types here.

The Beauty Parade: Here, my friends, we have a popularity contest. The communication style is definitely *People Person*, and the applicant everyone likes best gets the job. Well, it's almost that simple. The interviewer's motto is, once again, "We're a family here," and he will hire the person he wants to welcome to his work family. You will spend approximately a half day there, being shown around the company and being introduced to everyone—and I do mean everyone. When it's all over, the grapevine (which is alive and well in this organization) will have communicated the informal results of the poll to the employing manager and your fate will be sealed. Therefore, this is the time for gracious social conversation.

Strategies: Be nice to everyone; find something nice to say to, and about, everyone. Do not be controversial; do not "solve" problems (in this company, we don't have problems, anyway, we have "opportunities"). In other words, stay out of trouble. Remember, they're much more interested in whether or not they like you than in hearing about your qualifications. Do not commit the ultimate sin of "bragging" about your accomplishments. Interview attire should be somewhat relaxed but still professional. You should look and be approachable, not too stiff, and certainly not intimidating. "I'm friendly" is your motto for today. Like the Marathon, this is an interview people of mid-age generally handle very, very well—far better than most younger people, who may feel overwhelmed or confused by the social interaction.

That's it: the six interview formats you are most likely to face. Being prepared is half the battle. Enjoying the experience is at least another quarter; the rest is left to chance.

Final Words on Interviewing at Midlife

Age is an issue; to assume it is not is merely to evade the battle. You can't win the war without getting on the field.

Don't be surprised when you are interviewed by people who are far younger than you are; many of them will not have the benefit of your experiences, others will appear frighteningly lacking in knowledge. But don't assume either is true just because of their age. You may be happy to learn your interviewer is well informed and enthusiastic about her profession, and the conversation that follows may well be a delightful experience for both of you.

On the other hand, as companies come to rely more on e-mail and conference calls than on face-to-face interaction, I hear more and more stories about interviewers showing little regard for basic courtesies. You might be put off by the lack of relationship building that normally precedes getting down to the business at hand. This approach probably has nothing to do with how they feel about you, or your qualifications, nor does it reflect a negative attitude about your age. It usually shows nothing more than a lack of awareness or experience in dealing with people. If, however, you have any reason to believe they are concerned about your age, face it directly. In most cases, they will be afraid to bring the subject up, for fear of being liable for age discrimination, but not discussing it is not going to dispel their concern. Lay the issue on the table in a positive way and you can relieve their apprehension, then move on to more interesting discussion points. Try these icebreakers:

"At my age, I have the flexibility to travel extensively for the company."

"After being in management for so many years, I look forward to getting back to the technical side of the business, and focusing on projects."

"I think it's a great advantage for a company to have the credibility provided when someone my age meets new clients."

"I'm at the peak of my career, and I'm looking forward to new challenges."

Being "overqualified" is often the biggest barrier to someone mid-age being hired. I have never understood why an interviewer would assume that the person applying for the job is incapable of making his own decision regarding his potential for being happy there. It would seem logical that a company would do everything in its power to recruit the person most qualified to handle the job; however, professional recruiters, in particular, seem convinced someone they perceive to be "overqualified" will either be dissatisfied or will be immediately agitating for a promotion. Answering this concern, whether or not it is openly expressed, can sometimes prevent being eliminated from consideration.

"I don't believe there is any such thing as overqualified. Each job offers opportunities for professional development."

Regardless of the age of your interviewer, be aware that the details of your career are probably interesting to no one except you and your mother. The interviewer wants a general overview focused primarily on the last position or two. Offering anything beyond that is relevant only if it provides background not contained in recent experience, or additional substantiating evidence. Don't make the mistake of one of my clients who went for an interview at age fifty-six and was asked, "Tell me about yourself." He began with his first year of college nearly forty years previously! His point was well thought out. He wanted to show that even at that young age, he was targeted for management when he was chosen to represent his college dorm on campus policy issues. Indeed, it *was* the beginning of his very successful management career, but going back that far elicited little more than yawns. It also reinforced the old cliché that "elderly" people spend all their time talking about the good old days, hardly the way to dissipate the concern about age as an issue in hiring.

Which brings us to another point: Do not dwell on how you did things in the past or in the old company. Your interviewer's professional life may be much shorter than yours, and her interest is what you can do for her company, in the future. Nostalgia is great, but not in an interview. Note: It's hard to believe, but the Vietnam War was over nearly thirty years ago, and the Korean War and WWII predate many people sitting on the other side of the desk. It's hard to remember to keep references current, but make every attempt to do so.

Now we come to the very real danger of intimidating your interviewer. Would you like to work for your mother or father? Let's face it, you look like an authority figure. You fit the role of the boss much better than you do the employee, and that can be very intimidating. Far too often, interviewers face the disconcerting choice of hiring the person who is most qualified, or the person who makes them feel more comfortable. In such a case, the latter invariably wins. There are strategies you can use to overcome this potential age disadvantage:

- Check your interview outfit. Is it *too* powerful? Should you tone it down a bit?

- Show interest, energy, and enthusiasm . . . but do so in a relaxed manner. Leaning forward in your chair is better left to those under thirty-five. At your age, you're just plain scary.

- If you have an authoritarian, booming voice, tone it down.

- In like manner, be ready with a firm handshake, but don't rush at them.

- Men and women both need to feel comfortable shaking hands with people of either gender, and any age. Please, no fish grips or tentative attempts to avoid contact.

- Overfamiliarity is unacceptable, particularly with younger people. *No* friendly pats on the shoulder, hand tucked under an elbow to assist someone through the door (they're perfectly capable of handling this themselves, thank you), or sexist language.

- Watch terminology: hopefully, you are long past referring to women as "girls" or young men as "son." "Honey" or "dear" should be used only with someone to whom you're related (and even then you might want to check first!). Note: This applies to receptionists as well. Many a potential job offer was lost because the receptionist was offended by the interviewee.

- Ask questions and don't be afraid to say so when you don't know something. Nothing is as likely to create a comfort level and remove the threat of the interviewer feeling intimidated. It also shows you are open to learning.

- Be very careful not to let there be any doubt that you respect the role of the interviewer, particularly when he is significantly younger than you are. Let the interviewer lead the discussion. You are an equal partner in this exchange, but you are not in charge.

- Don't try to impress the interviewer; think of yourself as a consultant who is expected to bring wise counsel rather than a salesman trying to close a sale.

- Make it very clear that the prospective employer's interests are your top priority and that you expect to make him/her more successful, more productive, and happier by being there. Leave no doubt that you will be supportive rather than competitive; this is their main concern.

The "velvet hammer" is firm, solid, and sure, but never intimidating. Your approach should be the same.

CHAPTER EIGHT

Creating a Win-Win Situation

"Oh, I could show my prowess,
Be a lion not a mou-esse,
If I only had the nerve."
—THE COWARDLY LION, *The Wizard of Oz*

ALL of life is an exercise in negotiation. It's analyzing a situation and influencing people to get something done. Creating a win-win outcome takes confidence and conviction; you must believe ... completely ... in what you're after. You're also most likely to succeed when the outcome benefits the other person at least as much as it does you. Let the meek and subservient take note: The negotiating table is no place for a fainthearted lion, so screw up your courage and read on.

Who Has the Power?

In every negotiation, the participants' perceptions of where the power lies determines who actually has it. If you believe you have the power to get what you want, you're *probably* right, but if you believe you don't have the power to get what you want, you're *definitely* right. Job applicants frequently have the mistaken impression that the potential employer is in the power position. The reality is that hiring is a risky business. Employees are a company's most important assets, and choosing the right staff determines whether the company will succeed or fail, ultimately affecting the lives of every employee. The applicant has only himself at risk and with this flexibility comes power.

Don't be intimidated. Understand where the real power lies and use it effectively. It's also important not to want the job too badly. For if you do, you've already decided you'll take whatever is offered and you've given away all your bargaining chips. Negotiating the terms of your employment is a courtship dance and each partner must enter the marriage with trust and confidence, committed to the long-term success of the relationship.

Negotiate the Job

Jobs are negotiable: roles, responsibilities, resources, decision-making authority, advancement potential, professional development; nearly all aspects of the position are up for grabs. Although hiring managers must prepare job descriptions in order to post an opening, they rarely have a very clear picture of what they're looking for; it's more a general impression that takes shape as they interview applicants. That's why 50 percent of the people who are hired are the last ones interviewed; they are able to address all the issues that have surfaced in previous interviews.

Your goal is to be an active participant in creating the actual job description, ensuring you have the support system to succeed, for your sake as well as the company's. To do so, you need a very clear understanding of your strengths and skills and the work environment that suits you best. Your background gives you an excellent overview of the profession, and your research into this company and its competition should make you an expert on the potential for the position. Your responsibility is to negotiate the job responsibilities to match what you know you can bring to the company. This will no doubt require adjustments to the job description as it stands, so don't hesitate to explain the advantages of altering that position. Your ability to negotiate the position will determine your potential for success.

People assume that negotiating takes place after you are offered the job and that the goal is to walk away with a higher salary and more perks than were originally offered. The reality is that negotiations begin with the first contact between you and your potential employer. The relationship you develop during the process is a preview of the professional relationship you will have if you land the job. Once you have negotiated the job based on what you, specifically, can bring to the company, you eliminate your competition, and the law of supply and demand takes over. At this point they want *you* and no one else, and you have the upper hand when it comes to negotiating the details.

First you need a campaign plan, a marketing campaign with *you* as the product. Take time to prepare, using these questions as an outline:

Know your product:

- Where do you usually excel?

- What energizes you, makes you feel the most productive?

- What do you really care about? Skills are important, but building them on talents is the way to really get results. If you didn't need the money, what would you choose to do for free?

- Can you convincingly articulate what you can do? Your age gives you an advantage here, because you can back up your claims with accomplishments.

Know the market:

- Who needs your product? Who could benefit but is unlikely to know about your product?

- Where have products like yours been most successful? Have you researched the market?

- Can you provide specific evidence where your product has been used effectively: case studies, statistics, testimonials?

- What is your target market; who is the ideal customer?

The midlife career transitioner should know the market, but unfortunately, many have developed tunnel vision. Working in the same company/industry for twenty to thirty years can result in a very narrow view of the marketplace. Research is critical and so is objective self-assessment.

Know the customer:

- Why this customer? How do they fit the profile of your ideal customer?

- What can you do for them that no one else can? In other words, what will be your sales pitch?

- Have you researched the customer's market niche, competitive advantage?

- Where's the itch that you can scratch? Is there something they have failed to identify about the market that could give them the edge on their competition?

Age advantage is knowing the unique skills you bring to a job and identifying situations where you can be consistently successful. You should be able to hone in on such situations in this customer's operation. It's your job to spot them and articulate what you can do.

Who Has the Information?

Negotiation starts with knowledge. The successful negotiator is the one with the most information. A good rule of thumb is to devote three times as much effort to research and analysis as you do to the negotiation itself. The job applicant has the information edge because she controls the form and content of the information that flows into the potential employer's hands. The employer, on the other hand, is an open book, limited only by the amount of effort you put into researching. I've found that while the Internet is helpful in identifying job opportunities, it's invaluable in researching potential employers. You'll want to learn:

- What the company says about itself: marketing materials, annual reports, etc.

- What others say about them: newspaper articles, industry journals, competitors, vendors, customers, current and past employees.

- What the evidence and statistics show: market analysis, Dun & Bradstreet, annual report, etc.

- Observable characteristics: site visit, interaction of employees, cultural indications, community involvement, professional relationships.

The person who goes to an interview uninformed is at a distinct disadvantage. Getting the information edge means knowing what the other party wants or needs (not always the same), and *basing your negotiating strategy on getting it for them.* The more you know about them—priorities, communication style, values, goals, actual vs. published mission, competition, financial status, deadlines, and organizational pressures—the greater your competitive edge. Don't forget to use your network to ferret out this information. Your preparation must begin long in advance. If you're already negotiating a job offer, it's probably too late.

Negotiation Is a Process, Not an Event

Negotiating is a process that begins from the moment you make contact with an employer. The letter you write, the call you make, the résumé you submit, the application form you complete—whatever shape your initial contact may take, it sets the stage and creates the framework for the job negotiation. Regardless of the number of people interviewed, one person emerges as the lead candidate, the person they *expect* to get the job; the rest are comparison candidates. The ability to negotiate the responsibilities and the compensation package is largely dependent upon gaining the power position in this initial, subconscious ranking.

Who Has the Time Pressure?

Sometimes it seems, as Ben Hecht once said, that "Time is a circus always packing up and moving away." At the negotiating table, the person who appears to have all the time in the world generally comes out on top. The smell of urgency and panic gives away the competitive edge. Because the most significant concessions are made as a deadline (real or imagined) approaches, we really are masters of our fate if we can control our time. If you know the other party's deadline, and can be flexible with your own, you have a distinct advantage. As their time becomes short and their stress level rises, emotions take over, details are forgotten, and you're more likely to get what you want. Difficult as it may be, it's critical that you control your own sense of urgency in order to remain in the power position. Remember that time is one of your most powerful negotiating weapons. The longer the negotiation continues, the more you stand to gain.

Who controls the time? Companies spend an average of eight to twelve weeks in the job search process to fill lower-to-mid-level positions; sometimes several months for higher-level positions. When a new person comes on board, they can expect to spend another six months (some studies say a full two years) getting him up to speed. It's a cumbersome process that creates serious problems for the organization, but you can use it to your advantage. This time pressure is precisely why more and more companies are turning to contingent labor ("just in time" employees who are hired for short periods to fill specific needs).

What about the job applicant's time? Isn't her time just as valuable? It's tough to be unemployed month after month with financial obligations to meet and no way of knowing when it will end. Add the very real issue of age discrimination and, perhaps, outdated technical skills, and negotiating may seem like the least of your worries. But resist that line of thinking and control your impulse to rush things. Time is too important a bargaining chip to ignore. You must convince potential employers that you have the time and flexibility to wait for the *right* job. Assume your search will take several months and make plans to meet your financial obligations. Then be willing to take the risks necessary to negotiate with conviction.

The Negotiating Game

Think of negotiating as a game. First you negotiate the job by convincing the potential employer that what they really need is precisely what you have to offer. When the job has been redesigned to fit your strengths, your negotiating is half done. You are the preferred provider and all that is left is to settle the details of compensation. To place yourself in the power position, consider the following factors:

Cost/benefit analysis: What will be their reward if they hire you? How will you make them more successful and more efficient? How will you make their lives easier? What is the downside? How much time, energy, and company money have they wasted if they don't hire you?

CASE STUDY: Martha interviewed for a position with a health-care-insurance company as a benefits manager. A no-nonsense person with extensive experience, she was an expert in government compliance. She was reluctant to apply for the position as it only paid $45,000, a big step down from the $60,000 salary she earned in her last position. However, her severance pay was dwindling, her husband was unable to work, and she decided she'd at least go to the interview. It didn't take her long to realize that the senior management had no idea of how much trouble they were in. Inexperienced in this area of the business, they were exposing themselves to expensive lawsuits if they continued their current practices. Rather than accepting their $45,000 offer for the position, she negotiated a contract to bring them into compliance within six months for a bonus of $15,000. She also negotiated a pay raise at that time that would bring her up to her old salary. The company had no real choice, and they knew it. Ultimately, she saved their business and they were grateful.

Expertise: What do you bring to the table in terms of judgment, familiarity with a multitude of circumstances and people, and proven ability to handle diverse situations? This is invariably an age advantage. Presented properly, no thirty-five-year-old can compete with a fifty-year-old in this category.

> **CASE STUDY:** A high-tech manufacturing company won a $7 million government contract to provide a night-vision product to the military. They needed a marketing/customer-relations manager who could deal with the military and governmental red tape involved in the process and also keep peace among the company's divisions. It was a make or break contract for the company and Carl was a shoo-in for the job. He was calm, soft-spoken, but articulate, with more than twenty years in government contracting. His gray hair certainly didn't hurt! His very presence immediately reassured the top brass and he got the job.

Commitment: Generally, the person on the other side of the desk believes the midlife job candidate brings a work ethic to the job that's second to none. You will be expected to give far more than a day's work for a day's dollar and stick with the company through crises. Their investment in your training is bound to be repaid over and over, because unlike the thirty-something climber, it's unlikely you'll take the goodies and leave.

Credibility: The midlife job applicant has instant credibility. Everyone assumes that after decades on the job you know what you're talking about. To reinforce your image, use your vast network to put in a good word for you. Have them make a call; nothing is more impressive than a reference call from someone with firsthand knowledge.

> **CASE STUDY:** Joan was the public-relations officer for a leading West Coast university. She had a great relationship with the president, and when he left, she was devastated. She began looking

around for another position and set her sights on a prestigious private institution. She didn't think she had much of a chance, until she asked her former boss to make a call on her behalf. She instantly became the leading candidate, and six weeks later she had the job.

Persistence: It's never over till it's over. The biggest stumbling block for midlife career transitioners is their discomfort with asking for anything. They're much more comfortable on the other side of the desk. As a result, they're likely to take rejection very hard, very personally . . . and to accept it much too quickly. Before you count yourself out of the running, step back, consider the issues, and see if there is a way you and the company can work together to meet both your needs. It doesn't happen in one meeting. It requires negotiating with a partnership in mind, not just your own short-term gain.

> **CASE STUDY:** Bob applied for a job as CEO of a rapidly growing company. His background was primarily in finance with some human-resources experience thrown in. They were looking for someone with a strong operations background, so at the start he wasn't a leading candidate. However, he convinced them to give him a consulting contract for ninety days to evaluate their organizational structure, project their future staffing needs (to handle the anticipated increase in business), and devise hiring and training programs. He effectively halted his job search process to fulfill the contract, and in the end, he became the new CEO.

Focus on the company's success: The company isn't interested in what you want; they're focused on what they need and the immediate need is for their next hire to be successful, because that will make the company successful. It's just that simple. You should always bargain with this in mind.

Title, salary, perks are as important for the way they position you in the company as they are benefits for you. Anyone who believes compensation packages can be kept confidential is somewhat naive; the reality is that they, as well as the reporting structure, are major factors in establishing your credibility and authority (or damaging it!). Otherwise, you're setting yourself up for failure. Your aim is to balance the job responsibilities with what you believe you need to do the job. Showing that you are concerned about the company's success also goes a long way in establishing you as a member of the team.

CASE STUDY: Sean negotiated a lower salary for himself! He was being hired as VP of Operations for a rapidly growing company. They knew they needed someone of his expertise and were ready to spend the $125,000 (plus bonuses) it would take to get him, even though the president and the other three VPs were all on a $95,000 cap with shared stock options. They established this "cap" for a specified start-up period, agreeing to feed any profits back into the company. Sean rightly believed the others would deeply resent him for accepting a higher salary. Doing so would make it impossible for him to get the support he needed to succeed. He asked for a matching salary, believing that by working together, they could make the company successful enough to raise all their salaries within two years. He was right.

Convincing: At midlife, you can rightfully boast of decades of success convincing other people to do what you want them to do. Negotiating a job offer is no time to back away from the challenge. Logic alone won't win the day; the person across the table must believe her own life will be better because you are there. Remember: the company *wants* to believe. They've made you an offer; they're committed. They've spent a lot of time on you, and they certainly don't want to go back to the drawing table. There's also a matter of pride;

no one wants to admit to other people in the organization that they couldn't reel you in.

Sense of humor: Serious as the situation is, try to see the humor in it and enjoy the game. When you care too much, it shows, and puts you at a disadvantage. Develop a slightly bemused attitude (fake it if necessary!). Relax and even pretend you're negotiating for someone else, if that helps.

> **CASE STUDY:** Andre had been out of a job for eight months when he came to me. In that time, he'd had only one interview, and his confidence was shattered. He was dejected and desperate . . . and it showed. There was a panic in his voice, his eyes darted from side to side, and he constantly made little nervous gestures. It didn't matter what his qualifications were; at this point he was totally unmarketable. After we completed the self-assessment process, polished up his résumé, and developed a marketing plan, he seemed to regain some of his energy. He was cautiously optimistic . . . until his first interview, when he fell apart. We both feared he was back to square one, until I discovered how much he enjoyed community theater. I went to the library, checked out a volume of one-act plays, and he and I spent hour after hour reading parts, until he could fall naturally into a role with little preparation. Then we began role-playing interviews, pretending they were acting parts. It worked! I'm happy to report that today Andre is gainfully employed in a job he loves.

Competition: Both you and the potential employer must believe you have other options. Who wants to hire someone no one else wants? Regardless of qualifications, a competitive market means rising prices. These options may be actual or perceived. Whether or not other offers are on the table or only on the horizon really isn't the issue; believing they're out there is all that matters, because it puts you in control of your life. A word of caution: *do not say you have other offers* *unless it is true!* Nothing destroys your credibility faster than being caught in a lie, especially one meant to mislead your potential employer. So don't do it! If you actually do have another offer, and are at liberty to discuss it, however, it is only fair to give a second interested party the opportunity to compete. Just be sure to be respectful of both parties. You don't want to look like you're instigating a bidding war; it may come back to haunt you later.

Authority: Always negotiate with the person who has the power to make exceptions. It's almost always a mistake to try to negotiate with the human-resource representatives. They are the policemen of the organization. It's their job to make and enforce hiring/compensation rules. Go directly to your future hiring manager, the person who cares, whose life will be better because you are there. When you have reached an agreement, they will relay the information to the human-resources department. People at higher levels know rules were made for general circumstances; they were never meant to cover every situation (especially if it's to their advantage to make an exception!). Determine the risk the negotiator is taking and whether or not it's worth it to them, then "go for the gold."

Get it in writing: Promises or assumptions made in the heat of courtship are often forgotten. Ask for an offer letter. Be sure it includes all the details, not just benefits and compensation. It's those little things they promise, then withdraw, that you'll resent later. Does the offer letter include flexible work hours? Were you promised a laptop computer for work you take home? Will the company pay for parking? What expenses will be paid when you're traveling on company business? Will you earn comp time for it? Get these details in the letter and you'll both be protected. Be sure the person making the offer has the authority to make these concessions!

Negotiable Items: What's Up for Discussion?

When the job duties have been negotiated and you've reached the point of discussing a job offer, we can assume that both you and the company want to make this work. At this point there is a commitment by both sides to do everything possible to reach an agreement. Unfortunately, applicants are often afraid if they ask for anything, the other side will back away and go with their second choice. Let me reassure you that this practically never happens. If both parties negotiate in good faith, there's a 95 percent chance the process will go forward until you come to a mutual agreement. So, don't despair, and don't back away from stating your case.

There is much more to the job offer than salary, but monetary compensation causes more angst than any other issue. In my experience, the first side that mentions money loses. The company's job is to get the most work for the least amount of money; yours is to get the job you want for the most money. Your challenge is to convince them that you need/deserve/require the amount you're asking. This begins, of course, with the cost/benefit analysis; they have to believe you're worth it.

Let's be realistic. No employer posts a job opening without first deciding what they can afford to pay. They go into the negotiation with a specific range in mind and it is their duty to tell you what that range is. Quickly justify where you fall in the range, and go on from there. If you want the job, but sincerely believe you're worth more than they are expecting to pay, you're going to have to prove to them that they'll get their money's worth in return.

What you were paid on your last job has absolutely noth-

ing to do with what they are expecting to pay for the job they have posted! You are under no obligation to discuss it. In fact it's irrelevant. The question is whether they have a position for which they believe you are the best candidate, and whether you both believe you will be well served by joining forces.

Unfortunately, however, it is very likely you will be asked for your salary history and expectations, so you might as well be prepared. Here are some ways to avoid getting into a salary discussion too early:

- "I'm sure you have a range in mind and I'd be happy to consider that."

- "I'm more interested in challenges and opportunities than I am in a specific salary. Besides, I'm sure this company offers competitive compensation packages and we can discuss that when we both feel comfortable we can work together."

- If you're feeling particularly feisty, you might even say, "I'm sorry, but I believe that's proprietary information and not relevant to our discussion."

Once the company presents its offer, you can negotiate around it. As a general rule, you can assume companies will:

- Go up 10 percent from their original offer.

- Consider a "hiring bonus" of 5 to 10 percent.

- Be willing to give you a ninety-day review, and consider raising your salary by that year's annual raise percentage.

- Negotiate such things as stock options, bonuses, cost-of-living differences, cash in place of health benefits, etc.

Beyond the Paycheck

A total compensation package includes much more than salary, or even benefits, and sometimes those differences can more than make up for a salary offer that's lower than you'd hoped. The list below includes various forms of compensation and a rating of how difficult they are to negotiate.

1. Basic compensation: base salary, commissions, bonuses, corporate profit sharing, stocks, hiring bonus, company participation in 401ks.

You'll want to ask: *When are salary raises and bonuses given? Are bonuses determined by individual, group, or company performance? What is the potential for promotion? How long before someone at this level is considered for promotion?*

Very negotiable (except for 401k participation)

2. Health benefits: medical insurance (dental, optometric, etc.), life insurance, disability insurance.

You'll want to ask: *What are the deductibles? Will your family be included? If not, what is the charge for their participation in the programs?*

Rarely negotiable

3. Vacations, sick leave, personal days, holidays, compensation time. You'll want to ask: *When will you be eligible? Can they be combined? Are there rules concerning personal days or vacations taken before or after holidays? Sick days around vacation? Can these days off be taken "as earned" or must you wait a period of time? Can they be accumulated?*

Difficult to negotiate, but certainly worth a try, particularly the personal days and compensation time. This may be informally arranged with your manager, but if it is really important to you or if you expect to put in major overtime and want to be compensated for it, be sure to get it in writing.

4. Severance package, executive coaching: Discussing a golden parachute at the time of hiring is a little like asking for a prenuptial agreement. It's hard to admit the possibility that this marriage might not work. However, change is the one constant, so you're foolish if you don't negotiate some kind of severance agreement.

You'll want to ask: *When does it take effect? Is outplacement counseling included? What about health insurance? How about executive coaching?* The fact is most executives "make it or break it" within the first ninety days, but rarely do they fail because they can't handle the tasks. Rather, they stumble over interpersonal and communication issues, rooted in a business culture clash. Companies are very often willing to provide you with a coach for this critical period, a wise investment for the company and a real benefit for you.

Very negotiable

4. Relocation expenses: moving expenses, home sale and purchase expenses, temporary housing, trips to find housing, trips home during transition, job search assistance for spouse or adult children.

You'll want to ask: *How much money will be allocated for these expenses? How much is allocated toward each?* Those are the obvious questions. But don't forget to ask how long you'll have to make relocation decisions. Finding that right house or selling the old one may take much longer than you expect, and in the meantime, you and your family may be stuck in temporary housing you have to pay for, so be sure to clarify these issues. A spouse who works full-time won't be satisfied with the move until he or she has found a position. How will you deal with the expense of maintaining two homes and travel expenses in the interim period?

Very negotiable

6. Perks: company car or travel expenses, laptop computers, printers, cell phones, social-club fees, athletic facilities, clerical support, personal use of frequent-flier rewards, employee discounts.

You'll want to ask: The possibilities are wide open and you'll be amazed at what you can negotiate in this category. Most of these items come under the heading of discretionary in the budget, and decisions about how they're distributed are pretty much up to your boss. Get it in writing if it's really important to you.

Very negotiable

7. **Education/Professional development:** degree programs, professional continuing education, technical training (i.e., on computer systems and language courses) seminars, workshops. This category also includes professional organization memberships, conferences, journal subscriptions, books.

You'll want to ask: *Does the company support outside professional development? Will I be able to participate in educational programs during regular work hours? Will they be considered assets for future promotions?* Companies vary greatly in their attitude toward education and professional development. A manufacturing-company client of mine requires everyone in his organization to earn a minimum of forty credits a year and pays all expenses if the employee earns a C or better. Other companies consider such courses a personal expense and see no reason to give you time to attend them, so it's important to check.

Very negotiable

You Can If You Believe You Can

Negotiating is at least 50 percent attitude. Remember, you're going to live with these people at least forty hours a week for the foreseeable future, so it is imperative that the negotiating process create a positive relationship. This doesn't mean you should meekly accept anything that's offered, but it does mean the negotiation discourse should be respectful at the very least. Be prepared, assertive (rather than aggressive), and tactful, not only because you're more likely to gain concessions if you act like a reasonable human being, but also because these conversations set the tone for the honeymoon period that will begin on your first day of work.

Win-win negotiation is based on creating synergy, two minds sincerely focused on long-term solutions.

CHAPTER NINE

The Oldest New Kid on the Block

"Genius is an infinite capacity for taking life by the scruff of the neck."
—KATHARINE HEPBURN

YOUR adrenaline is flowing. You're at the starting gate and you're ready for the race. And then . . . you realize that even decades of experience haven't prepared you for the first day on a new job. You're older, wiser, aware of both the challenges and the obstacles that lie ahead. How will this job be different from all the others? Do you care as much about succeeding—or perhaps too much? Do you have the same need to prove yourself? What's at stake? Is it one more time up to bat and then it's over? Are your past successes enough to carry you through, or does anyone really care what you did before today?

First-day jitters are inevitable, whether it's your first day of kindergarten or your first day on a new job at age fifty-six. You're nervous and you want desperately to be successful. Failure is out of the question and mere adequacy isn't enough. You have to meet your own standards, the toughest of all.

The biggest challenge midlife career transitioners face is expecting that they can start where they left off. The greatest handicaps are failing to anticipate the learning curve and not realizing that success will depend more on adapting to the new company culture than on meeting the challenges of the position.

Assumptions can be your downfall. Don't assume:

- the company values will be the same as at the last company;

- the communication style that worked in the past will be equally successful here;

- you and the boss have the same goals in mind;

- your experience and background will be respected without question;

- you don't need to report your activities or the contacts you're making;

- you know what will work without bothering to consult with others;

- people are interested in what you think about how they do *their* jobs.

Yes, it's just like being the new kid on the block, in this case the *oldest* new kid on the block. You are expected to know more, but to be difficult and inflexible. People will be surprised that you are computer literate. Your peers (and even your boss) may be significantly younger than you are, and will be concerned about your willingness to take direction. Your work ethics will be admired, but sometimes resented because you set the bar so high for other people. People will ask your advice, and be resentful when you give it. You won't be terribly welcome when the gang goes for a beer after work, but if you don't come along, it may be interpreted as a snub.

It would be nice if you were welcomed with open arms, but that probably won't happen. It's your responsibility to make friends and your potential for success will largely depend upon your ability to do so because the support of other people is at least half the battle.

Winning Friends and Influencing People

As technology changes at an exponential rate, it creates a sense of urgency in the workplace. We have to make decisions today! Yet conventional wisdom holds that you shouldn't make any major changes in the first three months on a job because you simply don't know enough about the culture, the players, or the possible repercussions.

You've probably come from a company you knew well, where you had a strong support system. Unfortunately, you can't expect the same situation in your new company. Before you "rush in where angels fear to tread," let me tell you about a client of mine.

CASE STUDY: George L. had worked for one of the Baby Bells for twenty-seven years when he took early retirement and joined a small start-up company. He was thrilled to be a "real" engineer again, after spending the last twenty years in management. He quickly learned, however, that he was no longer familiar with the jargon, much less the technology. His first day at work, conversations were a blur of acronyms: SS7, SLEC, and CAP, shorthand that only remotely resembled anything familiar. In those first weeks, people often turned to him for support in heated discussions over policies and procedures. "Don't you agree, George?"

He'd nod sagely and respond, "Well, essentially." Carefully

avoiding commitments, he'd allow the discussion to move on around him and afterward he'd research the information. The next time the subject came up, he was armed and ready! After about a month he was not only familiar with the terminology, but good friends with his local librarian.

Ralph C. Medley was right! "Whatever your grade or position, if you know how and when to speak, and when to remain silent, your chances of real success are proportionately increased."

Making major decisions too quickly can get you into trouble, but it is equally important to become actively involved in the daily routine. Unfortunately, your coworkers may have the false impression that you are just there to collect a paycheck for a few years before retiring and aren't really committed to the corporate goals. Correct this misunderstanding immediately. My coaching clients often tell me they've been advised to show more enthusiasm. A laid-back communication style may give the impression you no longer have what it takes, or don't really care. *You* may recognize that the problem isn't a crisis, but that isn't much comfort to the person who thinks it is. Your calm demeanor may be interpreted as a lack of energy. Your new coworkers are expecting you to bring your considerable experience to the table, but they also want you to show the energy, enthusiasm, and determination it takes to get the job done.

A strong work ethic is one of the strengths of an older employee, but it can also get you in trouble if you don't take time to find out how it fits into the culture.

CASE STUDY: Merna M. is a 105-pound bundle of energy. She is a project manager par excellence, and when she takes hold of a project, she's like a dog with a bone. She'll do whatever it takes to get the job done, if that means working half the night, learning a new computer program, or handling details assigned to other people. That was the problem.

Merna went to work at a major high-tech company on a six-month contract to develop a marketing program for a new software program. Two weeks later, she was called in to the manager's office. The other contractors were complaining. They were upset on two counts: she was working extra hours without charging for them, and she was doing design work that was supposed to be contracted out. They had no complaints with her designs; the trouble was that when she took on additional work, it made them look bad.

When Merna explained the situation in our coaching session, she had already come to the realization that the problem wasn't just the extra work or her expertise; it was that she had been so focused on getting the job done, she hadn't taken time to understand the culture. Her commitment, loyalty, and hard work—qualities that had always been admired in the past—were not as important as being part of the team.

Not taking time to get to know the company, its people, and its culture is the leading reason new managers and executives fail. They don't fail because they don't know how to do the job. They fail because they leave bodies scattered in their wake as they move through the company like a tornado. Meeting with a coach once every two weeks provides a safe zone in which to talk about your concerns, explore communication and style issues, and analyze the culture of your new company. An objective professional's point of view can be critical to getting the perspective you need to handle this initial period with poise, building alliances and gathering people around you rather than scaring them away.

Company culture is simply "the way we do things here." When your way of doing things matches theirs, you're one of the clan almost immediately. If it doesn't, you may remain an outsider forever. Learn about the culture of the new organization by observing:

- Interactions: How do people greet each other, make casual conversation, show humor?

- Decision-making style: Do people make decisions and take action quickly or spend a lot of time thinking about the situation? Who is involved, what is the process?

- Style of dress: What do people wear in the office, to meet clients, for special celebrations?

- Communication style: What tone of voice is dominant? Do people interrupt one another in a free flow of ideas? Defer to special people?

- Familiarity or formality: Personal references, "small talk," questions about family?

- Mission and values: Are they real or token?

- Vocabulary: What's the "hidden language" everyone understands without expressing?

- Opinions: Are they openly shared or offered only when the boss asks?

- Organizational structure: Is there a difference between the one on the charts and the *"real"* one?

- Management style: Often there are two—the one they say they use *and* the one they really use.

- Preferred communication tools: Do people talk face-to-face, or send memos or e-mail?

Succeeding in Your New Career

Success or failure in a new job is usually determined within the first ninety days. You either make a place for yourself and establish solid working relationships or you destroy any possibility of doing so. Too many new managers are determined to make significant improvements immediately, believing such change will establish their credibility. Whether you are a new employee or a consultant, a good question to ask yourself at the very beginning is, "What are the company values that everyone understands, but no one talks about?" Those are the ones that can get you in the most trouble if you aren't expecting them. Consider these strategies to carry you through the critical early months:

Become computer literate. There is no place in today's companies where you can escape technology. Your comfort with computers can be a major factor in adjusting to the company culture.

CASE STUDY: Marvin W. was director of sales for a manufacturing company when hard times hit and he lost his job. A tall, good-looking man with a military bearing, he took the news of his job loss with great equanimity. He was sure he would find another position quickly and had no doubt of continued success. Months later, having declined several offers, he started to panic. Then the right job appeared. He sailed through the interview process and faced his first day on the job full of enthusiasm.

The first challenge he faced, however, was adjusting to a company culture that depended upon e-mail to communicate. His gift of gab and persuasive skills had been honed in face-to-face conversations, not writing memos. A computer illiterate, he quickly realized he had better improve his skills immediately and signed up for some classes.

Beware of alliance builders. It's easy to be swept away by initial overtures of friendship. Before you realize it, you may be on the wrong side of an epic battle. There are several types of people who reach out to newcomers. Some are genuinely friendly and merely want to make you feel welcome. However, it's difficult to separate them from less desirable types who are (1) willing to do anything to avoid work; (2) looking for support on a controversial issue; (3) eager to attach themselves, parasite style, to you and your position; or (4) looking for a friend because no one likes them.

Take time to get to know everyone before you make alliances, at least a few months. By then, you'll have had the opportunity to observe people in action, learn the history of past associations, and determine the direction you want to take. In the meantime, be friendly to everyone; just don't pick favorites. Play the political game, shaking hands on both sides of the aisle.

Don't be competitive. Your age advantage is that everyone expects you to have expertise and knowledge. You can afford to be generous. Ask for input from lower-ranking associates. You'll learn a great deal and gain their support at the same time. It's not your job to counsel everyone who comes to you, but for the first couple of months take time to listen and thank them for their input.

Establish a regular routine for discussions with your boss. Stay close to your boss for the first six months. Be sure you understand not just the goals of your position but the priorities. You can almost guarantee there will be more than one person can accomplish. At some point you'll have to make choices, and you'd better be sure you'll make the same choices your boss would make.

Being the oldest new kid on the block takes finesse, but remember Theodore Roosevelt's words of wisdom, "The most important single ingredient in the formula for success is knowing how to get along with people."

Provide psychological leadership. Share your vision with others. Your aura as an elder statesman will be enhanced in the initial days by focusing on strategy (big-picture goals and objectives) rather than tactics (details of implementation). See yourself as a mentor to others. The wisdom that is your greatest strength should make it possible for you to see things clearly and understand why others are mired in the trenches, digging themselves deeper into the hole. Your job is to help them see it for themselves.

Question conventional wisdom . . . particularly if it is your own. Internally challenge assumptions, yours and others. Ask yourself, "Is this myth or reality?" Again and again encourage others to question assumptions and welcome their ideas. Whether or not you act on their suggestions isn't nearly as important to most people as being heard. Work to establish a culture of big-picture thinking.

Recognize that trust must be earned. Have patience. In the long run, you save time, because trust can be destroyed in a moment, and once gone, it is nearly impossible to regain.

Take responsibility for your own training. Establish, by your example, individual ownership of learning. The assumption is that people become more set in their ways as they grow older and less willing to learn new things. Disabuse everyone of this idea immediately by being the first to read the latest book, to take a class in a cutting-edge technology, or to get the newest upgrade for your computer.

Find mentors. Ask for advice. People love to be asked, and when they give advice, they have bought into your success.

Spend a couple of months getting to know everyone, then find two people who will agree to mentor you for the first year. You'll be surprised how willing people are to serve in this role, partly because it's flattering to be asked, but also because they will invariably learn from the experience themselves. Put some careful thought into your choices! Take time to observe and determine which people in the organization have the most credibility. Be sure at least one has been with the organization long enough to teach you its history, to help you understand why things are done as they are. The other should be your most objective critic, someone who will tell you the truth when you need to hear it. Ask each to meet with you for an hour every two weeks. Come to your meetings with an agenda, ask questions, brainstorm current and future projects, and, of course, leave plenty of time for them to do what you've asked them to do: give you feedback and advice. This should always be a "free zone," where you both feel safe to say what you really think. One word of caution: Do not openly align yourself with your mentors outside of these sessions, or others in the organization may accuse you of "clique" building.

Don't expect the same standards from others as you do from yourself. If you are a high-action, energetic, highly productive person, patience is probably not your strong point. It's hard to allow other people to be who they are and to value them for it, particularly if they appear less invested in the challenges of the organization than you are. But the fact is, not everyone is willing or even able to give 150 percent to their work. Their work habits may be just as effective as yours, and badgering them or comparing your own efforts to theirs will do nothing to improve their contributions or increase their dedication. In fact, it will probably be counterproductive.

Have passion about your work but don't be too invested in either the company or the job. Allocate your time and emotional resources wisely. Are you working at a pace that's guaranteed to burn you out in a few months? Do you have life balance? Don't mistake activity for productivity. Stop and take stock. Is quantity or quality the real point? Are you running so hard out of fear, afraid of losing your new job, or because you haven't taken time to discover what else is out there? Have you become so narrow in your interests that you are missing out on a great deal that life has to offer? Set limits on your involvement in work, and when you reach those limits, go home to the rest of your life.

Encourage a free exchange of ideas. Don't "own" your ideas. Give them away without strings attached that imply, "I am my idea. If you believe it is valid, you validate me. If you believe it is invalid, then you invalidate me." That's a heavy price to put on an idea. Once you throw out an idea, it should become the property of the group, to be molded, enriched, embellished, or even set aside. Ideally, people lose track of which idea, or which part of an idea, came from whom. All they know is that they are excited about the result.

Be flexible but don't "overflex" or you'll wind up like the chameleon who tried to cross a Scotch plaid. He died heroically, trying to blend with too many colors at once. Focus on your strengths. Acknowledge your weaknesses and welcome input from others.

Broaden your vision. Take a close look at your own beliefs and ask yourself if you hold any prejudices. Now is the time to unload that baggage. Never criticize anyone without a constructive suggestion for how to improve the situation. The world has far more naysayers than it needs. What we really need are problem solvers and optimists who are willing to contribute their own time and talents to making things better.

No one is served by your pointing out one more thing that is wrong with the world. Why not use your wisdom, perspective, and experience to change what is wrong and celebrate what is right?

Don't internalize criticism. Listen and evaluate criticism objectively. Understand the criticism is about an action, not about you. Acknowledge the critic and absorb the lessons your conscience and your principles recognize as valid. Discard the rest and move on. You may need to explain your actions and ideas more thoroughly than you have in the past, but don't get hung up justifying yourself. This is a very difficult area for people who may expect too much of themselves and have very little tolerance for mistakes.

Be professional. What is professionalism? Everyone has a slightly different definition, but I think we would all agree it includes caring about what we are doing, and sincerely wishing the best for the organization as a whole. If you don't feel that way, you shouldn't be there. Not everyone has equal expertise, but everyone can be expected to *care*. It's fair to expect every member of the organization to be dependable and reliable. Anything less is unacceptable and should not be tolerated.

Focus on the results, not the credit. As a client once said, "The best part of being fifty is my mother no longer expects me to be president." When you can afford to share the applause, it's very easy to get support.

Extraordinary results require the support and contributions of extraordinary people. Give more, expect less. Build a team that can enhance your own capabilities. A large part of self-confidence is not only accepting yourself, but genuinely liking yourself. We spend so much energy in our youth creating an image, playing a role. What a tremendous relief it is to finally know your capabilities and be at peace with your limitations. Once you recognize that perfection is probably not attainable, you no longer have to camouflage your less-than-sterling attributes by surrounding yourself with deficient associates in order to look good. Suddenly it's more appealing to create synergy by surrounding yourself with talented people. *I'm okay. You're okay, and together we're dynamite!*

Look professional. Get a full-length mirror and use it. Would you turn to this person for good advice? Let's face it, appearance may not be everything, but it certainly opens the door. Pretend you are the casting director for a Broadway play. When that person in the mirror walks on stage, do you believe he or she is the part they're playing? Unless you plan on playing a character part, it may be time to upgrade your wardrobe, slim down that waistline, and get rid of the muttonchops and pancake makeup.

Do what you do best. Prioritize your efforts and invest your time wisely. Share the triumphs and everyone will want to be part of your successes. The depth and breadth of experience you bring to the workplace at midlife is a tremendous advantage, but it can turn into a disadvantage if you let your time become so fragmented that nothing ever gets done. Acting as a mentor to others is a generous, worthwhile effort, but don't let it usurp the time you need to focus on your own responsibilities.

Focus on being respected rather than liked. Leaving a company where you have worked for most of your long career can be a devastating experience. You leave behind not only the work you loved, but familial relationships: the parent surrogates, the lazy brother-in-law, the bossy sister, the little brother or sister you watch out for, the cranky neighbor, cousins you laugh and play with, role models you admire and look up to, and even the ne'er-do-well everyone covers up for. They were all part of a work "family," in which you knew your place and were accepted.

Starting over as a consultant, an employee, or even a business owner can be very lonely. It's easy to get distracted from work by subconsciously trying to replace old relationships. In the new world of work, everyone recognizes that work and family are separate entities. So, focus on professional relationships based on mutual respect and trust, not on emotional ties. There is nothing wrong with being liked, but as a need, it is misplaced and distracting in the workplace. In his inimitable style, Albert J. Dunlap, turnaround artist and author of *Mean Business,* bluntly states: "You're not in business to be liked. Neither am I. We're here to succeed. If you want a friend, get a dog. I'm not taking chances. I've got two dogs."

Learn the language of the new company and make it your own. Don't refer to past experiences to justify your opinions. At your age, people assume you know what you're talking about; don't drag the past along like a security blanket.

Be excited about your future and inspire others about theirs. Don't take yourself too seriously. The corporate ladder is gone, so quit climbing and enjoy what you are doing now, *now.* Have fun. Be open to the unexpected.

CHAPTER TEN

Owning Your Own Business

"Perfect freedom is reserved for the man who lives by his own work and in that work does what he wants to do."
—R. G. COLLINGWOOD

I F you've always wanted to own your own company, if you really have designed the perfect mousetrap, and if long hours and sleepless nights are your thing, owning your own business may be right for you. On the other hand, you should be aware that four out of five new businesses fail within the first five years. The success rate for franchises and acquisitions is much higher, but the risks and rewards can be equally volatile. It is a roller-coaster ride with the highest highs and the lowest lows . . . but it is never dull.

Midlife career transitioners are natural candidates for business ownership. They have the knowledge and experience for such an undertaking, and those who have lost jobs after long years in the same company are often reluctant to relinquish control of their lives to the whims of an employer again. Whether business ownership entails production and distribution of goods on a major scale or the desire for self-employment can be satisfied by becoming a consultant is a question that demands extensive self-assessment. Business ownership falls into three categories in addition to consulting, and although there are similarities, the characteristics and skills required to be successful in each are often quite different. Anyone who goes it alone is often referred to as being entrepreneurial; however, the term "entrepreneur" more properly belongs to someone who creates a new business, starting from scratch and taking all the risks inherent in such an endeavor.

Midlife is an in-between period when professional expertise and intellectual power are at their highest, but jeopardizing savings for a high-risk endeavor is not for everyone. Those who are most likely to take the gamble are people launching a business in their current field of expertise. Couples sometimes see owning a business together as a transition into retirement. Other people turn hobbies into businesses, hoping to enjoy life and make a living at the same time.

Franchises deserve serious consideration for the person who is adamant about being his/her own boss but isn't after the thrill of creating a business from the ground up. The financial risk is dramatically less if the franchise is carefully chosen because there's little in the way of experimentation. Theoretically at least, the format has been perfected and the franchise company will be as invested as the owner in ensuring its success. They'll provide you with a strict formula and procedures and require that you adhere to them. Depending upon the company, this should assure at least a minimum financial return on your investment.

The biggest drawback to acquiring an already-established business is the price you pay for "blue sky," the business reputation and customer base which, unfortunately, don't always transfer when you take over. You can require the previous owner to remain on staff for a period of time while customers come to know you, but this never seems to work out very well. This is partly because you will want to put your own identity into the business and this will automatically create a shift in your customer base. You're paying a huge financial price for very little long-term gain, in most cases, and you need to analyze very carefully whether it is worth it.

You may choose to purchase a mega-operation, but most midlife career transitioners who decide to go into business for themselves choose the small-business option, becoming part of the fastest-growing segment of the American economy. Some estimates show anywhere from two-thirds to three-fourths of new jobs created are in small business. A huge percentage are owned by women, the theory being that they can avoid the glass ceiling by building their own empires.

Small-business owners have the advantage of being able to make decisions quickly. They can dream up a new product or service and have it on the market almost immediately, respond to customer price and quality concerns, and even discontinue products without worrying about huge warehouses full of inventory. The flexibility and innovation inherent in small business appeals to the person who wants to see the visible results of her efforts, and who thrives on experimenting with new ideas without facing a big-business bureaucratic maze.

The self-employed consistently rate their job satisfaction as very high. Considering the failure rate, the long hours, and hard work, we can only assume that having control of your destiny makes it all worth the effort. The freedom to make choices also means being responsible for the consequences, good or bad. Being your own boss sounds great, but the reality is it usually translates into having dozens of bosses. Every customer, every vendor you owe money, every government regulator, and every lender is, in essence, your boss.

The percentage of business owners in this country will likely continue to rise as the Baby Boomers move through midlife. If one word characterizes this group, it is "independent." A strong self-image and personal confidence make them more willing to take risks than their older counterparts, the "elders," who are generally much more conservative.

People who choose to own businesses are often strongly motivated by personal values and a sense of mission. The mid-century mark has an alarming power to deepen motivations, and people at midlife have a natural desire to leave their mark on the world. A paycheck no longer seems enough; there has to be more value to the work they do. With advancing years come grandchildren and receding hairlines. Suddenly we have a heightened awareness of life's cycles and place higher value on the welfare of future generations. Regardless of the motivating force, owning your own business is not for everyone.

The Entrepreneurial Profile

Entrepreneurs are born, not made. They were the children in preschool who always popped up at the front of the line; the ones with purposeful strides who knew where they were going; the ones who had to do things a little differently from anyone else; the ones who were never afraid of anything (or if they were, they never showed it!).

Are you an entrepreneur? Do the characteristics that follow generally describe you? If not, and you still want to be self-employed, all is not lost. Purchasing a franchise is much more like belonging to a company than starting a new business. Purchasing an existing business falls somewhere in between (depending upon its size and reputation). Most people can find a type of business ownership that will satisfy their own American Dream.

Entrepreneurs are leaders, because they usually cannot (or will not!) be led. They don't always want to be in charge of other people, but they definitely want to be in charge of what *they* are doing themselves. When they were growing up, they always seemed older than the other children, more responsible, more sure of themselves. They took risks, but only if they believed it was worth the price. They had little tolerance for anything they considered a waste of time, and often found themselves butting up against authority figures who demanded adherence to the rules. As adults, they're still that way.

Entrepreneurs are generally healthier than other people, or perhaps they have as little patience with being sick as they do with anything else that doesn't hold their interest. They're perceived as strong and competent and other people often turn to them for help, something they don't always welcome but generally tolerate. They have things to do, and taking care of other people takes precious time away from their own work.

Entrepreneurs rarely play. Regardless of age, whatever they are doing is serious stuff, important "work." That is why you see children (entrepreneurs in the making) busily working on projects, building forts, directing (always directing!) neighborhood entertainments, and persistently asking adults for part-time jobs. As adults, they gravitate toward jobs that allow them to be independent, sometimes managing people but more often managing projects. Just as they did when they were children, they rarely choose diplomacy over honesty and don't hesitate to tell other people what they think of a new policy or idea, good or bad. Corporate politics are definitely not their strong suit, and they may even have missed promotions because of their bluntness. They have work to do, and they *never* suffer fools gladly.

Entrepreneurs don't need perks and care little for labels, designer clothes, name brands, or other status symbols. They are a world unto themselves. They do what needs doing, without regard for rank or privilege, whether it's scrubbing floors or running a meeting. They are certainly not concerned about getting their hands dirty, nor are they hesitant to talk to anyone, regardless of position.

Entrepreneurs are more likely to be considered friends by others than to consider others their friends. They are focused and purposeful, and may unconsciously ignore people (even those to whom they are closest) when they're involved in a project. The strength of their personalities usually draws people to them, but they don't always take time to develop or maintain relationships. They care little for praise, and may even seem a little puzzled by it.

Entrepreneurs see the clock as their enemy. There is never enough time. They manage to put twenty-six hours into every twenty-four with a waiting list of "to do" items. They thrive on challenges and are unaware when they are sacrificing themselves unnecessarily. In their own minds, they're responsible for everything, and they have to be reminded to let other people help them. They live by the motto, "If I do it myself it'll be done right."

Entrepreneurs synthesize information quickly. They see the big picture, instantly identifying causal relationships and moving to the goal. They prioritize and organize naturally, and other people turn to them because they appear to know what needs to be done. Interestingly, entrepreneurs rarely develop real expertise in any area. Perhaps they just move too fast.

Entrepreneurs are realistic. Their focus is on results. They size up situations quickly, recognize when something isn't going to work, and make adjustments. They have very solid egos, which are not invested in being right. They are as likely to use someone else's idea as their own if they believe it will accomplish the goal. They prefer to deal directly with people, without regard for protocol or layers of authority. They are usually not overly concerned with subjective criteria, but rather focus on visible results. They have little tolerance for philosophical discussions, which they consider pointless.

Entrepreneurs set high standards for achievement. Sometimes, they have a hard time dealing with family and close friends. In fact, they may be insensitive, forgoing personal relationships for pragmatic, down-to-earth solutions. They're unswayed by sentiment, and often unaware they've hurt someone's feelings. As business owners, their chief failing is a reluctance to delegate or share responsibility. As a result, they are not generally strong team builders. In many ways, entrepreneurs are loners.

Entrepreneurs are exciting to be around, almost always up. For them, the glass is always half-full. They are eternal optimists, eager for the next day to dawn. They have a zest for life, a curiosity and energy that is infectious . . . and sometimes exhausting.

Are you an entrepreneur? Do these characteristics sound like you? If so, owning your own business, whether an entrepreneurship, an acquisition, or a franchise, might be the perfect career choice.

A Word to the Wise

No one wants to start out believing they will fail, but it's a foolhardy person, indeed, who doesn't at least consider the reasons other people have failed in business ventures. Assuming that you are an entrepreneur by nature, and that your family has agreed to support you in this endeavor, what else should you be considering? Why do so many young businesses fail?

Inadequate financing: If financial security is high on your list of priorities, you should know that it is highly unlikely that you will take home a salary for the first eighteen months. Don't forget that you'll also be paying for your own benefits. Being sick or taking a vacation is something only people who work for someone else get paid to do. And those are just the personal costs. You will need financing to cover *all* business expenses for six to eighteen months. Getting the cash to cover these expenses is essential if your business is to survive its infancy.

Initial start-up costs are invariably much higher than you anticipate and there are bound to be costly mistakes such as ordering supplies for a job that is canceled at the last minute; *or* hiring help through an agency at exorbitant costs; *or* getting a letterhead print job back that has to be replaced because of a typo; *or even* natural disasters like ice storms that keep people away from a grand opening. A general rule is to anticipate that anything that can go wrong, will. You'll be grateful when something goes right. Sock away any income for the next emergency.

CASE STUDY: The Carlino family opened a small neighborhood pizza place. Word of Mama Carlino's incredible sauces spread quickly and it wasn't long before they had a line going out the door. Unfortunately, the equipment they bought was too small to handle the volume. They had also signed a lease on a facility that could seat only forty people at a time, so they had no way of growing the business to meet the demand. There was no ready cash to expand and no possibility of additional financing.

People soon tired of waiting to be served, and as quickly as customers had come, they disappeared. The Carlinos failed because they hadn't built in the flexibility and financing to handle success.

Lack of management experience: Running a business demands not only business sense but solid experience. Owning a business is the big time, not the place to learn on the job. Hiring, training and managing people, handling finances, dealing with government regulations, tax and legal issues, production and delivery (whether you are selling products or services), customer service and billing: the list goes on and on. At least 25 percent of your time will be spent in handling the "business of the business," substantially more in the beginning.

Lack of ability/willingness to market/sell: So, you say you have an innovative product or service the public is just waiting to buy? How do you intend to tell them about it? The quality of the product is often not as critical to its success as the marketing of it. If you are not an expert in this area, please hire someone who is. It's not as easy as it sounds. Advertising agencies, public-relations firms, and marketing gurus are available everywhere, but finding someone who understands your product and the potential market, and who can work well with you, is quite another matter.

These are the three big causes of business failure. Others include:

- limited market for the product

- seasonal/topical market

- poor-quality product

- poor location

- reliance on too few accounts

- promising more than you can deliver

- poor communication and people skills

- lack of expertise in the field

- lack of commitment or energy to put in the hours it takes to be successful

- lack of structure and procedures to operate efficiently

- focusing on the competition rather than the customer

- poor pricing: too high or too low

- inadequate computer skills

- failure to collect bills

- failure to target your sales efforts

- not realizing the customer—right or not—deserves to be heard

- failure to stay current in the field

- losing your sense of humor

Assessing Your Entrepreneurial Fit

Evaluating yourself on these characteristics will give you a general idea of how you fit the entrepreneurial profile.

There is no magic score that tells you whether or not you should give it a try, but this profile will help you to identify your strengths and weaknesses in order to determine if owning your own business is really a good idea.

	That's Not Me					That's Just Like Me				
1. I'm a natural leader, people have always looked to me for direction.	1	2	3	4	5	6	7	8	9	10
2. I have a great deal of management experience.	1	2	3	4	5	6	7	8	9	10
3. I am in consistently good health, and rarely take a sick day.	1	2	3	4	5	6	7	8	9	10
4. I prefer work to play.	1	2	3	4	5	6	7	8	9	10
5. I generally see the big picture and don't get distracted by the details.	1	2	3	4	5	6	7	8	9	10
6. My family is very supportive of my going into business for myself.	1	2	3	4	5	6	7	8	9	10
7. I am very objective about people and am not swayed by emotions.	1	2	3	4	5	6	7	8	9	10
8. I am very self-confident and well balanced emotionally.	1	2	3	4	5	6	7	8	9	10
9. I am highly ambitious, a self-starter who gets things done.	1	2	3	4	5	6	7	8	9	10
10. I am known for having excellent people skills.	1	2	3	4	5	6	7	8	9	10
11. I have successful marketing/sales experience.	1	2	3	4	5	6	7	8	9	10

	That's Not Me								That's Just Like Me	
12. I have adequate financing to cover business and personal expenses for the first eighteen months.	1	2	3	4	5	6	7	8	9	10
13. I never mind getting my hands dirty and am willing to do the "grunt work."	1	2	3	4	5	6	7	8	9	10
14. I have done the market research to determine that there is a need for this product or service.	1	2	3	4	5	6	7	8	9	10
15. I have expertise in the field.	1	2	3	4	5	6	7	8	9	10

If you have a score between 130 and 150, it's a "GO!"

If your score is between 110 and 130, you are certainly a strong candidate for entrepreneurship.

If your score is between 90 and 110, look for partners or associates to fill in your weak areas.

Below 90, perhaps you'd better consider working for someone else, or at least focus on franchises, where you will have lots of support.

Butcher, Baker, or Candlestick Maker

Should you create your own business, buy an existing business, or purchase a franchise? Which fits your own nature and reflects your personal style? Regardless of the product or service, size or nature of the operation, this initial decision is the most critical in determining your potential success. Certainly, knowledge of the field, a clearly identified need for the product/service, and adequate financing are major factors in the decision, but it's easy to get caught up in the excitement of owning a business and rationalize your decision without factoring in whether you really enjoy doing the work. Visualize a typical day after you've been in business for six months. Forget about how exciting it was planning the wedding, is this marriage going to work?

Is **entrepreneurship** your style?

If so, *you are a creative person who is easily bored with routine. You're happiest when you're learning and growing. You want to do things your way. You look forward to new challenges and enjoy change. You are a "hands-on" person who likes to be involved in all aspects of projects. You see the big picture quickly and jump in to do what needs to be done, without regard for status or role. You are almost always optimistic, a real "can do" person, with great confidence in your own abilities. You are a natural leader but probably not a very good follower. You often take on more than you can handle, but somehow always get it done.*

Starting your own business is a very risky endeavor. If you follow history, you have about an 85 percent chance of going out of business within the first five years. Survival up to that point will depend a great deal on how much you're willing to contribute of your own time and money. What kind of toll will it take on your health, your marriage, and your relationships? You will have innumerable sleepless nights; the question is whether they will be because your head is full of new ideas for the business or because your stomach is full of ulcers. For the right person, it will be the most fun you've ever had. For the wrong person, it can be a disaster.

Is **franchise** more your style?

If so, *you are not a risk taker. You like to be sure of things before you step in. You prefer to work in teams where everyone has a specific role and responsibility. You are generally not the chairman of the group, but can always be counted on to do your part and do it well. You like established policies and procedures, statistics and data. You like to spend a certain amount of time working alone and are considered hardworking, reliable, and stable. Independence is important to you. You like to be able to control your time and plan ahead. You don't particularly think of yourself as creative or innovative.*

If you are a very creative person who wants to do things "your way," you're going to feel stifled and controlled as a franchisee. You won't last long as you begin to realize how little change you can make. You are your own boss, but it may feel more like being a manager for someone else. Risk will be minimal, depending upon the franchise company, and your chances of financial success will be as high as 80 percent, because your customers are coming for a name they know. "Growing the business" will be a matter of tightening and tweaking, rather than creating.

Is **buying a business** what you have in mind?

If so, *you like winning. You are competitive and driven for success. Making a lot of money may be important to you, but even more than that, you want to be in charge. You have probably been a successful manager most of your career and feel confident discussing the legalities of business ownership, profit-and-loss statements, ROI (return on investment), and stock options. You know the product or service well and have complete confidence in your ability to run the operation. You consider yourself a good judge of people and may be somewhat hierarchical in your style. You are not necessarily creative, but you are definitely recognized for efficiency and bottom-line results.*

Too often someone buys an established business and finds that they simply don't have the determination or "take charge" attitude to win the confidence of the employee body or carry the operation through the initial transition phase. Just because the previous owner was successful doesn't mean you will be. Purchasing the "blue sky" of a customer base and projected sales is often nothing more than dissipating vapor after the new owner takes over. The style of the previous owner, the customers who were loyal to him/her, and previously satisfied and productive employees all undergo serious change under new ownership. You have to hit the deck running, with a clear concept of where and how you will take the company forward. You have to be ready to create new markets to grow the business, or make up for the customers who fall away. Take a look at why the previous owner decided to sell before you make your decision to buy. Take an especially close look at any owner who says he or she is retiring, because people who own their own businesses rarely retire from them if things are going well. These are the most common reasons businesses are on the market:

- The market for the goods or services is declining; i.e., sales are down.

- Competition is moving in and taking over with new products.

- There is no money or talent for research and development.

- The location is no longer good.

- Boredom: the fun of creating the business is gone.

- Death, ill health, divorce, family emergency.

- A partnership has broken up.

The right fit is entirely possible but it requires (1) honest self-assessment, seeking out and listening to people who know you well, both personally and professionally; (2) extensive informational interviewing with people in business for themselves; (3) serious research of a number of businesses, including market and customer profiles; (4) full support from your family.

Once they have the green light, the born-to-be entrepreneurs charge forward, confident and bursting with energy, with rarely a look back, because the path ahead is so natural, the sense of freedom so empowering, the thrill of the game so exciting that there's nowhere else they would rather be.

Evaluating the Idea

Deciding to go it on your own is just the first step. Do you have a great idea for a business? No matter how determined and willing you are to devote all your energies to making it work, the bottom line is you must have a product or service other people want to buy. Where do the successful ideas for business start-ups come from? Some are natural spin-offs from previous occupations or hobbies, some are based on observations you or your friends have made as consumers, some are totally off-the-wall. You'll substantially increase the probability of success if you first evaluate the business idea by writing down detailed answers to the following questions.

- Describe the business idea in fifty words or less.

- Why is this product or service needed? What products or services are now in existence that would either benefit from or be replaced by yours?

- What is the market for this product? Are there enough potential customers? Is it a common product or service, or one that is limited to a specific audience?

- What are your specific qualifications that will make you a credible producer/marketer of this product or service?

- What are your personal goals in the next five years? What role does your business idea play in your life goals?

- What major barriers do you anticipate in making your business successful? How do you plan to overcome them?

The Business Plan

The importance of developing a thorough Business Plan cannot be overemphasized, for the difference between success or failure is often determined by the planning you do now for the long term. It includes such things as market niche, your customer base, how you'll incorporate the business, financing, operating procedures, and staffing. The Business Plan is also the primary documentation you will need to secure financing. Lenders must be convinced that you are not only capable of running a business but that you know specifically how you'll go about it.

Writing a Business Plan is both an art and a science and there are many books on the subject. A good source is the Small Business Administration (SBA) office in your area, which will have numerous pamphlets and books as well as regular classes you can attend. The Service Corps of Retired Executives (SCORE) volunteer their time and expertise and are an invaluable source of advice and counsel. You can reach them through their Web site: www.score.org or through the SBA.

In the following sample of a Business Plan table of contents, I have also provided a short explanation of each element.

Business Plan Table of Contents

Executive summary: Provides a brief overview of the business, its mission, market niche, long-term goals, and operating methods.

Background: Explains why this business is needed and its place in the general market. Describes your own professional background and the particular skills and background of the people who will hold major positions.

Business charter: Describes the company in detail: the product or service, market niche, marketing approach, and specific productivity and financial goals.

Competitive analysis: Provides a detailed description of your competition and describes the position your company will fill. Analyzes market share and outlines a profile of the target customer. Includes market trends and statistics and estimates quarterly sales for the first three to five years.

Marketing plan: Describes how you will market the business: strategy, outside resources, advertising and promotion, trade shows, sales staff, etc. Includes projected costs.

Development of product: Describes research and development of the product or service, time lines and methods for developing future products. Includes background information about people who will be doing the development, whether or not it will be outsourced, and estimated costs. If manufacturing is involved, it includes projected length of time the product will be viable in the market, equipment costs, etc.

Financial plan: This should be a very thorough analysis of the projected methods of financing the company as well as ongoing procedures for record keeping. Includes cash-flow analysis, profit-and-loss statement, break-even chart, ROI (return on investment).

Operating plan: How will you run the company? This section should include details of staffing, hours, how you will make and deliver the product or service, and the facility.

Schedule: Provides a detailed schedule of events, including market research, development of product or service, attaining financing, hiring staff, securing facility, promotion, and opening of business.

References: Letters from people who have significant experience with you in related professional areas. Includes letters from potential customers who explain why they believe your product or service will fill a need in the market and why they have confidence in your ability to deliver that product or service successfully.

Legal Forms of Owning a Business

WARNING: To tackle the legal and tax issues involved in owning a business you absolutely must rely on the services of an attorney and a tax accountant who specialize in this area.

You must have a formal organizational structure for your business in order to operate legally. You'll need professional help to register your business and ensure you've followed legally mandated procedures. Do your own research first, however, as you want informed advice, not private tutoring. Go to your meetings with questions and a specific agenda. Remember, lawyers and accountants charge by the minute, whether by phone or in person.

In general, there are three legal forms for operating a business:

Sole proprietorship: You own the business in totality: the assets, profits, and potential liabilities. The buck begins and stops with you. It's generally a rather uncomplicated way to start and to operate a business, as your personal and business lives are essentially combined. This is also a potential disadvantage, because of the personal legal liability if someone should sue you (i.e., because of an injury sustained in your facility or from a product or service you sell).

Incorporation: Your business is a separate legal entity, with articles of incorporation and bylaws, that pays taxes, assumes liability, earns profits, and pays salaries. One form of incorporation may be more appropriate for your business than others. The liability issue is the major reason people choose this option. There is also a certain credibility inherent in incorporating, and it can be comforting to know your personal assets are kept separate from the business. People normally assume there will be a tax advantage, which is not always true, so be sure to check it out.

Partnership: You and at least one other person own the business, sharing assets, liabilities, and profits and losses. Whether this "marriage" is a good one depends in part upon the relationship between you and your partner, but also on how carefully the contract is written. Sharing talents, skills, and financial obligations can be great, but be sure you have a clear understanding before the business opens.

Some questions to consider before deciding:

How much control do you want to have in determining the direction of the company and making day-to-day decisions?

Can you work this closely with anyone else? Is the original idea yours? Will you be comfortable sharing the results when the business becomes profitable? How will the duties be distributed? Too often, one person comes up with an idea, takes on a partner for their expertise in marketing or sales, and later, resents sharing the profits. On the other hand, a partnership is a good way to get the expertise you need and share the risk, but still be able to assume the role of president or CEO.

What will happen to the company if you become sick or even die?

If you choose a sole proprietorship, who is going to take over until the business can be sold? If one of the partners suddenly dies, the other is there to manage the business. Remember, unless you have very clearly defined rights of survivorship, your partner may be forced to sell the business just to pay off your inheritors. Conversely, the latter may receive nothing if the business goes directly to the surviving partner. These are important issues to settle at the time you establish the business. Incorporating is generally a simpler way to ensure continuity and survival of the business if one of the owners is unable to continue.

Will this company be dependent upon your continuous involvement? What about vacations, sabbaticals? What plans do you have for succession? Will the business still be profitable if you decide to work part-time?

Owning your own business can be physically exhausting. Your plans must provide some kind of relief. The tendency in sole proprietorships is to bring in family members to help out, but this means you can never take vacations together. Who will take over when you want to slow down? This is a distinct advantage of partnerships, particularly if both of you are qualified to handle all aspects of the business.

Are you and your family comfortable with the potential liability?

Business ownership means accountability and responsibility far beyond what you faced as someone else's employee. Are you up to it? Sleepless nights are probably the most common complaint of business owners. Whether it is worry about monthly cash flow or long-term solvency, financial responsibility knows no hours of the day or days of the week. Legal liability is greatly reduced by incorporating, but the nature of the business itself largely determines your exposure. Still, the risk is there and you and your family will need to balance the stress this places on your lives with what you hope to gain. This is a very personal decision and one you should not undertake without their full support.

Are you confident in your ability to run the business, or to pay for the talents and skills you need to be successful?

Have you ever been completely in charge? If you have never had total responsibility for managing an operation, or even a project, think very carefully before proceeding. Running your own business is not a good place to start. Have you successfully hired and supervised people? Are you skilled in sales and marketing? Are you a good budget manager? "No" answers to any of these questions should give you pause. Finding people with the talents and skills you need is very difficult, particularly when you are just learning the business yourself. It is not impossible . . . just very challenging. You need to be aware of pitfalls and have people in mind before you take the plunge.

How comfortable are you working alone? It's lonely at the top. Would you prefer to have someone to share ideas, triumphs, disappointments, and responsibilities? Who will be your support team?

This is a more serious issue than you might imagine. People who come out of corporate life are used to having others around them, whether it's someone to bounce ideas off, to help out in crunch times, or merely to share a joke. We're social animals, at least to some degree, and we miss this camaraderie. It just isn't the same when you are dealing primarily with employees, customers, vendors, and investors, each of whom wants and needs something from you. A partner is also a companion, another reason people decide to go into business together. Often they do so with a friend, close associate, or even a family member. This has good and bad points, not the least of which is risking the personal relationship when you don't agree or discover you don't work well together.

What are your plans for financing the business?

Inadequate financing is the primary reason businesses fail. You must be able to survive six to eighteen months without income. Have you figured out how you can do this and still provide for your own living expenses?

What are weaknesses in your personality that might benefit from close association with someone who has these strengths?

Your past personal and professional experiences will tell you where the problem areas are. Look over annual evaluations, seek straight-talking advice from friends and associates, and take some career assessment tests. Most of all, be honest with yourself. Going into business alone means you have to be all things to all people all the time. Sure, you can hire people to cover specific areas, but the bottom line is, you're it. Are you comfortable with this or should you be considering a partnership?

Professional assistance in areas where you do not have expertise will pay for itself over and over. In addition to an attorney and a tax accountant, you might want to consider hiring the services of consultants in such areas as business management, finance, marketing, and manufacturing. Get the services you need, but don't become overly dependent upon them, or you might find you're spending much more of your own time and money than is really necessary or useful.

Financing Your Business

As a business owner, concern about finances will never be very far from your thoughts. Regardless of the amount of responsibility you had in corporate life, nothing really prepares you for the awesome responsibility of being totally accountable for the financial stability of a business. Knowing that people you have hired are dependent upon their jobs, thus on you as their employer, can keep you awake at night. No one ever has enough money; it's a matter of juggling needs and borrowing from one well to keep another from going dry. Lack of capital to make the smart decisions on stocking or expanding your operation, on hiring the expertise you need, getting the training you need, or for advertising is a constant frustration. You'll spend more time checking cash flow than you used to spend on leisure activities.

It all begins with acquiring funding to start the business. Relying on personal savings is risky, not just because you may lose it, but because you will tend to limit your business decisions to the size of your resources. It takes time for most businesses to establish a positive cash flow. Mortgaging property or borrowing from friends and relatives can limit your ability to make coolheaded, objective decisions. Other sources to consider include venture capitalists, small-business investment corporations, silent partnerships, suppliers (who may agree to give you credit), banks or savings-and-loan companies, even state development commissions. Of course, the size and complexity of your business will determine in large part which of these sources is the most logical. Can your business start small and grow slowly? Or will you need a major outlay before you can open the door? The answers to those questions may quickly point you in the direction of one or another financing source.

Your approach to potential investors will depend upon what you are offering them in return. Unless the money is a straight gift to you, investors will expect some kind of return on their investment, usually from interest or stock in the business.

Investments based on **Mission** (e.g., belief that the product or service will help society in a way that matches the investor's own values) gain the support of groups such as foundations, nonprofit agencies, philanthropists, state development commissions, churches, universities, and even family and friends. The cost of using these funds can be amazingly low if you are able to convince investors that their own interests will be well served.

Investments based on **Equity** mean the person or group providing the funds ends up owning a part of the action. They take the risk along with you, and are sometimes willing to invest with a lower rate of return if the potential for making money from the operation is high. You will need to convince them of your ability to make a success of the business, to assure them that the product/service is marketable and that they're bound to make a greater profit than they could expect to make from another investment.

A word of caution: Before you go after equity investments, realize that these investors will expect to be involved in the decision making. This is particularly true of venture capitalists, hard-nosed professionals who will make your old boss look like a pussycat. This is no place for a novice. Be sure the lines of authority are clearly established in writing, and don't make the mistake of basing the return on gross rather than net profits. This is a typical mistake of first-time entrepreneurs, who are so grateful to get financing they fail to scrutinize the details. The reality is that no matter how carefully you plan your start-up and operating costs, it will cost substantially more than you anticipate. Professional venture capitalists are well aware of the propensity of first-time business owners to underestimate costs. By basing their return on gross profits, they ensure that they get their money, regardless of what happens to you. More than one owner has ended up with no take-home salary, paying personal expenses and taking out personal loans to pay off debts owed to investors. One former client told the story of his retail business that looked great on the books but amounted to no profit for him at all; it was all going to the investors. He eventually sold the business (to one of the investors) to get out from under.

Investments based on **Securities** are essentially loans, usually from banks or other loan agencies. The Business Plan is important to all investors, but for security investments, the credibility of the plan, and your own as the business owner, will depend on the thoroughness with which you present the details of your projected operation. Not only does the business have to make sense as an investment, but anyone who considers loaning you money must have absolute confidence that you will be able to manage the business successfully. They will want to know that you have "skin in the game," that you are putting your own financial resources at significant risk, as well as contributing sweat equity and time. First-time entrepreneurs often mistakenly believe investors will be willing to put up money strictly on the assumption that the owner will give professional expertise and time to running the business. This is rarely true. A security investor will nearly always expect you to put up collateral in the form of property or stocks, to cover any potential loss. You will also need to fully disclose your personal finances in detail.

Marketing Your Product or Service

Are there customers for your product or service? How many? How will you reach them? Are they aware of this product or service? Do they use it regularly or only occasionally? If they use it only occasionally, will you have to market to them each time, or will they remember you? What is the possibility of increasing the customer base? Will need or demand for your product or service likely increase or decrease over the next five years? Why? What factors will influence demand? Who are your competitors? What kind of funding and affiliations do they have? How well do you know these people or companies? Are you known in the field?

The questions go on and on. Market analysis is a serious business, one you might consider hiring a specialist to do. There are few elements of owning a business that require more specialized expertise, and none are more critical to your success. You will certainly have opinions and insights, but this is no place for an amateur. It's simply too important, so unless your field is market research, go to the experts.

Regardless of the time and money you put into your product or service, it is worthless to you as a business owner unless someone buys it. In most cases, this will depend as much upon your ability to get the information to the potential customer as it will on its value. Advertising works. However, it doesn't work just because consumers learn about the product or service. It works because it makes them believe they will (1) look more beautiful, (2) run faster, (3) be more successful, (4) entice a lover, (5) make money, (6) be admired or respected, (7) be happier, (8) worry less and play more. In other words, it isn't just what the product or service can or will do, but how it will affect their lives that really counts and pushes them toward the purchase.

Marketing to the wrong consumer is a waste of money. Even more harmful, it gives the business owner the false sense of security that she's doing something that will lead to sales, so she neglects to look for other marketing opportunities. Don't confuse marketing and sales. Marketing deals with the big picture. It means:

1. Understanding every potential attribute of your product, its strengths, its weaknesses, its competition.

2. Developing a profile of the target customer. What interests them, how do they spend their time, what do they enjoy, what are their concerns and insecurities, their hopes and dreams? How do they spend their money?

3. Analyzing what aspects of the potential customers' lives would be more successful, happier, more productive *if* they had your product.

4. Devising written and visual messages that most clearly present the attributes of your product/service in language that reflects the values, image, and goals of that customer.

5. Using market research to find the medium that will most effectively reach the target customer. How and where do they get information? What medium has the most credibility with them: Internet, print, radio, TV, billboards, professional newsletters, personal letters, recommendations of friends or business associates.

6. Getting your message to the right people through targeting and niche marketing. Go for quality, not quantity, at first, at least until you establish some credibility. Then expand carefully in order to maintain a solid reputation. When all is said and done, word of mouth is still the best kind of marketing, so let your satisfied customers be your best ads.

A sale takes place because someone believes, for whatever reason, that a desire or need will be met by acquiring a product or service, and decides that the cost is worth it. Whether or not this proves to be true will determine whether or not they become repeat customers. You as a business owner cannot look forward to long-term survival unless they do become repeat customers, so avoid the temptation to grab a quick sale when you know it is not in the best interests of the customer. Invest in the future by building strong customer relationships built on trust. Tomorrow's sales will always depend upon the way you treated yesterday's buyers.

The myth of the better mousetrap that brings customers flocking to the door is often just that, a myth. Whether or not your doorway is flooded with buyers will depend upon three factors:

- a credible product

- whether or not people need or want the product

- getting the information to the customers in a manner that makes them want to buy it.

The facts are simple, the implementation much more complicated. If marketing and sales are not your strengths, your business is unlikely to succeed unless you get professional assistance.

To Be or Not to Be . . . an Entrepreneur

Owning your own business is one of the most exciting, challenging, overwhelming, frustrating, and humbling experiences you can possibly imagine. It pulls together every talent and skill you can muster and tests them on a daily basis. When you succeed, you're on top of the world—but just for a moment, because if you are a true entrepreneur, you will soon be off again to find a new challenge. Being your own boss makes it nearly impossible to ever again work for someone else, because regardless of the outcome, you have experienced the thrill of creating something that other people choose to buy. It is a heady, addictive power, for you neither have to ask permission nor forgiveness. You are the boss and you make the rules.

It is not uncommon for entrepreneurs to fail one or more times before succeeding. The advantage you have in starting your own business at midlife is that you've made your mistakes while working for someone else. You bring a wealth of experience, including observations of how other people succeeded or failed in their endeavors. Judgment, common sense, and the ability to evaluate opportunity vs. risk add substantially to your potential for success. You're older, more likely to seek advice and counsel, and you have good professional contacts to help you over the rough spots. The number of new business starts increases each year, and with the proliferation of home offices wired with the most up-to-date information technology, the twenty-first century will no doubt see a significant number of people moving from corporate life to retirement via entrepreneurship.

CHAPTER ELEVEN

Consulting

"Work not only transforms the environment by building bridges across rivers and cultivating barren plains; it also transforms the worker from an animal guided by instincts into a conscious, goal-directed, skillful person."

—MIHALY CSIKSZENTMIHALYI, *Flow: The Psychology of Optimal Experience*

COACH, guide, instructor, mentor, teacher, pathfinder. A consultant is a counselor and adviser valued for wisdom and trusted to provide guidance in matters of great importance. At midlife, you are probably qualified and deserving of the faith others will place in you. That's half the battle; the other half is deciding whether or not you want to assume the role.

Consulting as a profession is growing by leaps and bounds. The first wave followed the downsizings of the late 1980s and early 1990s when companies eliminated their most experienced workers in a widescale cost-cutting exercise. It flooded the job market with highly skilled workers, and many turned to consulting when they couldn't find jobs.

The second wave came in the mid-1990s as companies

discovered the advantages of contingency labor. Workers, they realized, could be hired for special projects or during times of increased need and then let go, eliminating the cost of salaries and benefits during downtimes. Consultants filled the gaps. Employers were confident these proven midlife troubleshooters would solve their problems and then be on their way. An enormous industry evolved.

Consulting is a form of business ownership that provides independence, respect, flexibility, the opportunity to do what you know and love, and minimum financial risk. It offers the potential for great financial gain and it is the optimum way to transition from full employment to retirement. In fact, age is an advantage and many consultants retain their professional roles well into their seventies and even eighties.

On the other hand, consulting is a lonely business. You'll often be working by yourself without a support staff, feedback from peers, or the exchange of ideas that is an integral part of working in an office. Most often you'll be talking to people who are paying you amazing sums of money to be brilliant and they expect their money's worth.

Are you a highly disciplined self-starter, someone who does not need external guidance or reassurance? As a consultant, you are on your own and that is a challenge few people are comfortable handling. It is also difficult to separate yourself from the job and to take time for leisure activities or your family. When you are your own boss, there is always more to do. You'll select which contracts to accept, very likely projects that truly interest you, so you may *choose* to spend excessive time on them. Personal relationships invariably suffer.

The most frustrating part of being a consultant, particularly for someone who has come from a position of authority, is that you must rely on your persuasive powers to get things done. No one *has* to do what you recommend—in fact, you have *no* power over them. You may have the perfect solution or program that will guarantee success to a client company, but if they fail to implement your ideas, they *and* you will fail. Consulting is as much a matter of sales as technical expertise. It's more important that the client believe you can make *them* successful than it is to convince them of your own success. They also have to believe their needs are as important to you as they are to them. Just being right is not enough. Exceptional communication skills are as critical to a consultant as expertise.

On the other hand, clients tend to grow dependent upon their consultant. Once you are in, it is relatively easy to stay there. You can become indispensable, if you:

- focus on their priorities

- are always available

- have a specific niche that does not warrant a full-time employee

- exude an aura of confidence

- approach their projects in an open, thoughtful manner

- make them more successful

Profile of a Consultant

The opportunities for consultants are growing at nearly exponential rates. The key is to anticipate work that needs doing, and no one is better able to spot those needs than someone who has been in the field for twenty years or more. If you are willing and capable of handling the "business of the business," and equally willing and able to market your services, the opportunities are enormous. Consulting means owning your own business, and to be successful you must have the characteristics of an entrepreneur. In addition, you must be able to answer each of these questions with an un-qualified, "Yes!"

- *Do you generally see the big picture? Do you synthesize information quickly?* Consulting is not about short-term, stopgap measures; it is about problem solving that has long-range effects.

- *Are you comfortable communicating with people you don't know well?* As a consultant, you will be plunged into new environments, dealing with people who have different viewpoints, backgrounds, values, and priorities. Can you deal with such shifts?

- *Are you able to work effectively without a support staff?* You may decide to hire an assistant, but you will certainly not have support from multiple departments as you did within a company. If you have a question, you'll have to research it yourself or hire outside expertise.

- *Can you work alone? Are you someone who identifies solutions on your own, or are you most effective brain-storming with others?* Consulting is lonely. You certainly can't admit to the client that you don't know the answer. Who can you talk to?

- *Do you prefer hands-on or theoretical work?* Remember, as a consultant, you will have to convince others to implement your ideas, rather than do it yourself.

- *Do other people think of you as a leader?* To succeed as a consultant, you must inspire confidence; people must instinctively follow your advice.

- *Are you a self-starter? Do you anticipate what might need to be done and prepare for it, rather than wait for direction?* As a consultant, you're on your own. You are the boss *and* the employee.

- *Do you have a reputation for integrity and standards that others aspire to achieve?* Your clients will be entrusting their own futures and their companies to you, and they must have complete trust in you.

- *Can you deal with irregular cash flow?* Regardless of the size of the contract on hand, the fear that it will be the last is ever present. Like ants scrambling for crumbs, consultants find it difficult to ever sstling for work, regardless of how well they are doing.

- *Are you current in your field?* A consultant is only as marketable as the last problem he solves, and that means continuing your education. It requires incredible willpower to bypass a lucrative contract to make time for a class, professional conferences, research, and reading, but it is essential if you hope to maintain your marketability. You must continually be learning, growing, and developing new services and products if you hope to keep ahead of competitors.

- *Are you process-oriented rather than task-oriented?* Managers either do, or supervise the doing, of tasks. Consultants provide models for how the work should be done and excel at facilitating, gaining consensus, negotiating, analyzing, and teaching. Although a consultant must have expertise in a specific area in order to win the contract, in many ways she must function as a generalist rather than a specialist. Success is based on big-picture thinking, planning, and organizing. It is determining the ultimate goal and figuring out a way to get there in the most efficient way possible. It also means looking for opportunities to broaden the existing contract to include other areas of the organization. A one-shot consulting contract does little for your long-term success. When you get into a company, you want to become part of it. As one consultant said, "When I get in there, I own the company."

Why Hire a Consultant?

Companies need the expertise of consultants in order to:

- obtain specialized expertise

- introduce new concepts, programs, or methodology

- develop skills; provide ongoing training

- improve internal communication

- provide objective evaluation of company operations

- update technology or management style

Establishing your niche as a consultant means identifying the specific needs you can fill and being able to communicate them to the client. In many ways, it is an educational process. In most companies, the elimination of mid-level management positions has had unexpected consequences in the following areas, each of which provides an opening for consultants:

1. Knowledge of the company's history

2. Management experience and skill, which provided continuity, ongoing mentoring, and development of young talent

3. Long-range perspective

4. Intuitive problem-solving skills based on past experiences

5. Effective methods of interacting based on long-term working relationships

People at mid-age who become consultants usually come out of management and they bring back to an organization what it lost when it cut these positions. If the consultant is also technically up-to-date, he offers an almost irresistible package.

Your Future Client's Checklist

If you have decided consulting is right for you, the next step is to understand the business from the client's perspective. Most often you'll be hired for a particular project and a specified time period. Occasionally, this becomes an on-going relationship that can last for years. Remember, it's risky bringing a stranger into a company, someone who will probably want to do things differently, or who may introduce technology that requires additional costs. Consultants are "change agents" and change is never easy, so the client knows they will have to deal with employee reactions that range from enthusiastic support to sabotage. Therefore, they need to be very sure that (1) it's really necessary to hire a consultant, and that (2) you are the right one. They need assurance before they make their decision and will look for answers to questions such as:

1. *Why do I need a consultant? Do we have the expertise to handle the job in-house? Should I be hiring someone who has these skills on a permanent basis?*

2. *What is the scope of the work? How will the consultant and our company evaluate the completed work? Is*

there a time clause? Penalty for going over the target date? If we choose to extend the contract, is the consultant going to be available?

3. How will I evaluate whether my business is more successful because of the time and money I spend on a consultant?

4. How much can I afford to spend in terms of: money? time? personnel?

5. Is this consultant compatible with our staff? Will he/she be given respect and support?

6. Will I get what I need in terms of feedback? Will the consultant be flexible and willing to accommodate my changing needs?

7. Is my proprietary information safe? How do I know the consultant won't take our trade secrets to my competitors on the next consulting job? Will I "own" the research and/or creative work the consultant does for my company?

8. Will this contract be the consultant's first priority? Will subcontractors be used? In what areas? Will I have right of refusal on them?

9. How will my employees react to news that we're hiring a consultant? Will it send a negative message about my confidence in their abilities that will affect their productivity? Would it be better to offer them the opportunity to get training or education to handle this work?

10. How will the consultant gain a clear understanding of our organization? Does the consultant plan to spend time on his/her own getting to know us, our culture, the way we communicate, and how we operate, before beginning the work?

11. *Is this a "cut and paste" job, where the consultant brings programs/solutions/training "off the shelf," or will the work be specific to our organization? If the former, what reason do I have to believe that programs designed for other organizations will work here?*

12. *What have this consultant's other clients/customers had to say about her/his integrity, reliability, follow-up, and on-time production? How do they describe their experience? Would they use her/him again? Is their relationship with this consultant ongoing? Why or why not?*

Consulting Business Options

A consulting business doesn't have to be a one-person operation, although that's the way most people start. Another option is to go into business with someone whose expertise is compatible with yours—either someone who shares your expertise or who complements it in a way that broadens the appeal of your business. A third option is to form an alliance or consortium relationship with other consultants, which can substantially increase your marketability without increasing your financial obligations or limiting your flexibility. The fourth option is to join an established consulting firm.

A word of caution: Be sure the consultants with whom you align your business and reputation share your ethics, integrity, and level of expertise, or you will rapidly lose credibility. It's a little like a marriage; compatibility isn't always enough to carry you over the rough spots. You must also share the same values and have mutual respect. A real advantage of the consulting business is independence. You can help a client identify a problem and find a solution with no corporate bureaucracy slowing you down. You can move in and out of operations with very little notice. You may lose all this by teaming up with someone else.

Here in brief are the pros and cons of the options you face:

Go it alone

Pro:

- Independence.

- Flexibility.

- You alone choose the projects you'll work on, have control over how they are handled, and determine the quality of work.

Con:

- Isolation.
- Every idea must come from you.
- Inability to handle larger contracts.
- Small size generally means low visibility, a marketing obstacle.

Partnership

Pro:

- You'll have someone to share ideas.
- Ability to handle more diverse and larger projects.
- Partner can round out or complement your expertise.
- Clients are likely to be more comfortable knowing someone else could take over if you were unable to continue.

Con:

- Unexpected incompatibility.
- You may disagree on how to handle projects.
- You may have different priorities.

- You'll need to reach consensus before taking on a project.

Affiliation/consortium
Pro:
- Expands your market capabilities.
- Provides additional expertise in areas where you may be weak.
- Gives you close association with other professionals.

Con:
- Ultimately you have no control over the way your colleagues represent you and your business.
- You share profits.
- They may not always be available when you need them.

Join an established consulting firm
Pro:
- An already established business with policies and procedures in place.
- Instant credibility.
- Marketing may be done by someone else.
- Less financial worry.
- Professional peers available for brainstorming and discussing ideas.

Con:
- Less flexibility.
- May be expected to work regular hours.
- May have little choice of projects.
- May be on billable hours (work directly billed to the client) for compensation, profit sharing.
- Group will evaluate you and your work.

The best way to learn which option fits you is to talk to people who are already doing it. Consultants are amazingly accessible, generally willing to talk about what they are doing, how they got started, and even to give you advice on how to start your own business. Remember, they are advisers, counselors, teachers, and guides. It just comes naturally to them to share their wisdom.

Whichever option you choose, make it legal and binding, and don't even consider starting without a complete business plan! Hire an attorney and a tax consultant to review your plans. If you decide to go into a partnership, have the attorney draw up a partnership agreement and be sure it allows for every contingency you can possibly imagine.

Legal Paperwork Concerns

DON'T FORGET TO ADDRESS RIGHT OF SURVIVORSHIP AND BUYOUT IN YOUR PARTNERSHIP AGREEMENT! If one of you dies, what happens to income from ongoing contracts? Do your heirs receive a percentage? How will you divide the work? Will both of you do the marketing and sales or will one be primarily responsible for bringing home the bacon? An imbalance in responsibilities may cause problems later. After the partnership acquires a number of clients, the person doing the majority of the delivery may come to believe the salesperson isn't necessary. What about expanding the partnership? If one of you wants a nice, comfortable, semiretirement living and the other wants your firm to become one of the Big 8, there's trouble ahead.

There is also the question of incorporating your business. The pros and cons vary according to state laws, your priorities, the potential size of your business, and potential for liability. Your attorney will have the best advice on this score.

Financing the Business

Financing your consulting business is relatively straight-forward compared with buying a franchise or launching a manufacturing business. The fact is, banks and other loaning institutions are simply not interested in lending to neophyte consultants. There is no collateral in the business, and the chances of its succeeding are too dependent upon one person. In short, you are on your own, unless you can talk family members or friends into staking you. Nevertheless, planning the financial side of your business is just as important as it is for any other business, as is developing an appropriate record-keeping system and staying in close contact with your tax attorney.

Licensing the Business

Licenses to operate a business, as well as to consult in your area of expertise, vary from state to state and from field to field, but you can generally assume they're mandatory. A business license is usually easy to obtain, with more or less bureaucracy depending upon state regulations. Note: Be sure to research the licensing regulations in each state where you expect to do business! Some professions have extensive licensing requirements, particularly those where public safety is at stake, such as engineering or construction.

Where You Hang Your Shingle

If you are planning on transforming a former employer into your major client, you probably are not interested in establishing an office. You'll be on-site most of the time, and when you aren't, your extra bedroom can house your records. If you are seriously planning to market your services to other clients, however, you need to consider the issue of where you will work and how your office will affect your efficiency and credibility.

Clients don't often visit the consultant's office—usually you visit them. But when they do, it is important to present a professional impression. An executive office suite may be the answer. These offer receptionist and message services, conference rooms, and presentation equipment, all at a very reasonable price. Be sure to meet the neighbors and check out the qualifications of the clerical support.

If you decide to set up your own office, remember that doing so increases not only your costs but also your responsibilities. Now you have a lease, utilities to pay, and an office to manage. Leasing decisions alone are a serious business. For example, signing a five-year lease will lock in a monthly cost, and once you sign on the dotted line, you are committed. One consultant discovered two years into a five-year lease that the city was going to tear down two nearby office buildings, eliminating parking in the area and creating a traffic nightmare, not to mention the dust, noise, and general chaos. No one wanted to move into that mess, so he was unable to sublease the space and move to a more desirable location. He was stuck and he saw his business suffer when construction began.

Marketing Your Consulting Business

Marketing is an unrelenting challenge. Nothing will matter much unless you are able to get clients to buy your services. The bottom line is that it eats up at least 25 percent of your time, probably much more in the beginning.

Here are some places to begin:

Past employers: Many midlife transitioners take the work from a former employer with them. It's the easiest way to get business, but there are some drawbacks.

1. Your client may continue to view you as an employee and treat you as such. So much for prestige.

2. They may expect to pay you what they consider a fair price: your last salary, minus benefits, vacation days, even fifteen minutes off for coffee. You'll be paid strictly for "billable hours," and at that rate you will be earning from 30 to 40 percent less than the total compensation package you left behind: not a good deal.

3. They know you too well. You'll rarely get the benefit of the doubt.

4. You'll get very little slack when problems arise, little praise when you do something well.

5. Working for a former employer can lull you into a false sense of security. If, and when, it is over, you'll be out of work unless you start looking for other contracts right from the start.

6. You really aren't learning what it's like to be a consultant; you are an amorphous employee/contractor.

Networking contacts: Networking is the foundation of a consulting business. There is simply no way to be a successful consultant without word of mouth. Testimonials, either on a brochure, letters, or other marketing materials, are extremely valuable. Ask your referrals to explain how you have helped them to be more successful, rather than just talking about your knowledge and expertise. Results are what count.

Armed with referrals, your next step is to approach potential customers. One way to get appointments is through *cold calls*. It's a rare consultant who doesn't spend a substantial amount of time "smiling and dialing." The most difficult part is getting to the right person; the next is the damage to your ego when you don't (or are rejected when you do). I advise clients to send an introductory letter with their marketing material first.

When you are creating your networking list, don't forget to include professional associates outside your field who know of you or your work, or who may simply think highly of you. Vendors, your former employers, customers, consultants with whom you have worked in the past, and leaders and members of professional associations to which you belong—all are good contacts.

Direct mail is rarely successful for consultants unless it is specifically targeted to an audience you have already determined wants and needs your services and who can and is willing to pay for them. Otherwise, this kind of shotgun approach is expensive, unlikely to produce results, and will only distract you from the kind of networking that brings in clients.

Advertisements are a mixed bag. Paid advertising is very expensive and there is absolutely no question it is a sales pitch. Whether or not this is damaging to your credibility probably has to do with the nature of your consulting business. Is it customary for consultants in your area to advertise?

However, under the heading of advertising fall some tools that work very well for consultants. One is **newsletters.** They are almost expected of consultants and help create the image that your business is about teaching, advising, and counseling. Writing and publishing a newsletter is not a task to be taken lightly, however. If it is to represent you and your professional expertise, it must be done well.

Don't overlook a simple and required method of advertising, the **telephone directory**. Obviously, your clients need to be able to reach you, so you will need to have your business name in the book, anyway. Taking out a display ad makes it easier for the clients who know about you to find your number and it is a direct way to reach the first-time shopper.

Aside from networking, perhaps the best way to advertise your business is through **public speaking**. Professional conference organizers are always looking for speakers. Other public-speaking opportunities include local and regional service clubs, chambers of commerce, churches, associations: the list goes on and on. If you are a good speaker, you may well find yourself declining invitations to speak in order to be sure there's time to actually deliver your services.

Regardless of how you go about approaching prospective clients, it's important to create and maintain a consistent image. It should reflect who and what you are as a person as well as identify your expertise in your field. Too sleek an image is just as damaging as one that is too unsophisticated.

Bringing Them Back a Second Time

Referrals are the heart of any consulting business. What a good feeling to learn a client liked you well enough to ask you back! At that point you have arrived! How is it done? Through:

- Consistently doing a good job.

- Nurturing good relationships; people buy from people they know and with whom they are comfortable.

- Adding unexpected value to your services free of charge.

- Making the clients and their staffs look good.

- Being available; staying in touch.

- Guaranteeing your work; if something goes wrong, make it good or refund the fee.

- Being genuinely interested in the clients and their businesses.

- Asking for referrals; provide a methodology that will make it easy for them.

- Listening more than you talk; you'll learn a lot and they'll know you care.

- Being sure they are aware of all the services you offer.

- Referring them to someone who can do a better job when a project doesn't fall within your expertise.

- Asking for feedback and giving them yours: you are in this together.

It's always easier to sell to someone who is already a client. If nothing else, they will return your calls! They know your work and feel comfortable with you. Their staff know you and you understand their needs. Hopefully, they feel good about their increased success as a result of your last contract with them, and are ready to sign on for additional services. The assumption is that you will continue to enrich your repertoire, so you have more to offer them. Yesterday's product is like yesterday's news: out-of-date and irrelevant. Stay current and let your clients know they can rely on you to keep their businesses on the cutting edge.

Delivering the Services

In general, people who choose to become consultants do so because they have recognized expertise in a field and full confidence in their abilities. However, too few really consider how much of their time will be involved in the very serious and time-consuming work of running a business. The major incentive to become a consultant is the opportunity to do what you love. It's easy to become disillusioned when you suddenly realize you are spending far less time at it than you did when you worked for someone else. To be successful, a consultant must enjoy the challenge of operating a business, or hire someone else to do it, something few beginners can afford.

Consulting is a process, with eight defined steps:

1. Defining the problem/challenge

2. Qualifying the client

3. Contracting

4. Analysis

5. Presenting the findings and making recommendations

6. Delivering the service

7. Evaluating the project

8. Follow-up

Each of these steps presents its own challenges.

Defining the problem/challenge: Your first challenge is to determine:

- What *is* the problem or challenge?
- Can it realistically be solved?
- Are you the person to solve it?

Your second challenge is to reach agreement on the objectives and a realistic scope for your consulting services.

> **CASE STUDY:** Johnson Electric is a retail/wholesale seller of electric supplies, primarily to the construction industry, with forty-five branch offices throughout the western U.S. A family-owned business, the company had been in operation for sixty-five years. Many of the employees had been there well over thirty years, and remembered Mr. Johnson, grandfather of the current president, fondly. They told stories of him visiting people in the hospital, sending turkeys for Thanksgiving, and never forgetting a birthday. Young Jim was quite another matter. A recent MBA had given him the confidence, if not the experience, to run the company, and when his father decided to retire, Jim was given his opportunity.
>
> Jim was determined to change the culture of the organization. Demand for their products was growing rapidly, and he saw the opportunity to increase the business at an exponential rate if he could transform the company's image from a great place to gather for morning coffee into a high-action, efficient place for contractors to do business. He called in a management consultant.
>
> In the initial meeting, the consultant quickly recognized that there was no quick fix to the problem. To change a company's culture is a process, not an event. It couldn't be done overnight, and reasonable expectations and time lines had to be agreed upon. Some long-term employees would be uncomfortable with the new culture and many would probably choose to leave. Jim would have to let others go and this was bound to create morale issues. What Jim saw as a simple, straightforward consulting project was much more complex than he realized.

Consultants are constantly torn between accepting a contract based on the client's analysis and expectations (which the consultant knows to be unrealistic) and risking losing the contract to a competitor by telling the truth. One very successful consultant has solved the dilemma in her own mind by establishing the motto "Give them what they want until you can convince them of what they need." In other words, get in the door, gain their trust, and then lead them to the solution. Remember, if they could solve the problem themselves, they wouldn't need you. They are hiring you for your expertise and you have an ethical responsibility to give them the best advice you can offer.

Qualifying the client: This means determining if you can do the job and if the client is willing and able to invest the necessary time, money, and personnel. Neither you nor the client is well served if you provide a solution—however brilliant—that the client doesn't apply, for whatever reason. A great deal of the "qualifying" will be done when you complete the process of defining the problem/challenge. How many of their employees' work hours will be taken away from production? Will they be lasting changes? No consultant can be effective without total commitment from the top of the organization and buy-in from the management team to implement your recommendations long after you leave.

Contracting: A contract is a legally binding agreement to provide services at a specific cost. It is normally preceded by a formal proposal in which you define the project and present your plan for completing the work.

A general rule of thumb is to keep the contracts as simple and clear as possible. All contracts should include:

- Scope of work: *Exactly what are you committing to do?*

- Time line: *When will the project be completed? Is there a schedule for completing intermediary steps?*

- Deliverables: *What will the client have "in hand"?*

- Final outcomes: *How do both parties know when the project is completed?*

- Client responsibilities: *What role will the client play? Who will be involved? What resources will be available? When and how will they be provided?*

- Change-order procedures: *If the client decides to make changes to the contracted services, what will be the process for presenting, reviewing, accepting, and pricing them? Who will be involved in the decision? Can you refuse to accept a change order you deem distracting or even de-structive to the total project?* This is critical!

- Payment schedule: *Fees, advances, purchase-order for-mat, time allowed from invoice to payment, penalties for late payments, and methods of determining changes in costs* must *be clearly defined. Establish a policy to stop work if payments are late/not paid.*

A handshake is a wonderful way to seal a bargain, but don't begin a consulting project without a signed contract.

Analysis: This is probably the most important part of your work as a consultant. It begins with a clearly defined state-ment of what you perceive the problem to be. It should be short, to the point, and clearly understood by all parties. A good way of establishing a perspective on the problem is to determine the dynamics for change.

- Why is there a need/desire to do something, to make a change?

- What is the driving force? What is the problem to be solved or the potential advantage to making a change? Why is it worth it to spend the necessary resources?

- What is currently preventing change from taking place? Who or what might block change?

Never expect everyone to be supportive of changes you propose. To deal effectively with their reactions, it is very important that you understand at the very beginning who might object and what they might find objectionable. You also want to know who the advocates might be. You can investigate these issues by interviews, questionnaires, document analysis, and direct observation. Be sure to clarify whom you are permitted to interview during this process. Never assume. Your list may include vendors, customers, board members, and competitors as well as employees.

Presenting the findings and making recommendations: A summation of your findings should be presented in a formal report, usually with accompanying overheads, flip charts, or other visual aids. This is your opportunity to renegotiate the scope of the problem and to clarify any issues that might have emerged.

The final portion of your report should outline the steps you will take to solve the problem or, if your contract was limited to this analysis portion of the work, the steps you propose the client should take to solve the problem. Use this opportunity to market your services for the implementation stage or related projects. It is not unusual for the consultant to discover new factors or even entirely new issues during this stage.

Delivering the service: Yes, it's true, it's not until you reach the sixth stage (of eight!) that you are actually doing what you know best and enjoy most: delivering the service. Here I have very little advice to give, for you are the consultant and your expertise is what has gotten you to this point. I would point out some basic truths, however:

- *Always deal with everyone with complete integrity.*

- *Keep your word;* if you say you will be somewhere, be there on time, prepared, and ready to deliver.

- *Communicate, communicate, communicate.* You may be doing a superb job, but keep the client informed every step of the way so they will feel as good about what you're doing as you do.

- *Keep confidences.* There is never any excuse for revealing proprietary or confidential information.

- *Be professional,* in every sense of the word, at all times. You are not being paid to be someone's best friend; you are being paid to do a job.

- *Be willing to say "I don't know" when you don't.*

- *Keep your perspective and your sense of humor.*

Evaluating the project: It's never over till it's over, but when it is, both you and the client will be best served by a thorough evaluation of your services. In the best-case scenario, the project ends on time, on schedule, and on or under budget. The reality, however, is that something or other is bound to have strayed from the original projections. Either you or the client may be responsible or it may just be that new issues have emerged that require a change in plan.

Typically, you will provide an evaluation form to the clients that includes all aspects of the original contract agreement, including the status of specific deliverables. They will complete it; you will review their comments with them and then include this feedback in your final report. In this report, you should also provide recommendations for future improvements/additions and additional projects that might enhance the client's potential for increased success.

Follow-up: A consultant is only as good (or successful) as the last successful project. Combine this with the fact that the easiest marketing prospects are current clients, and you will welcome the opportunity to return for pro bono follow-up sessions. From your perspective, it's an opportunity to evaluate your own work, to determine if the fix really took, and to reestablish your relationship with the client. Let's face it, it's also a great excuse to come knocking on their door again.

Transformation from Employee to Consultant

Consulting is a gratifying finale for a successful career. It is the opportunity to share what you have learned with people and companies who can benefit from your experience . . . and be paid for it. It offers the potential for great financial rewards, though most consider it for reasons other than economic. It is not uncommon for my clients to choose consulting simply to avoid a job search, but there are much better reasons, including the flexibility to work when, where, on what, and for whom you choose and the opportunity to work independently on work you love.

Whatever your reasons, it is not an endeavor for the faint-hearted. Nor should it be undertaken lightly as a pastime while you decide what else you might want to do. People are likely to translate the statement "I'm a consultant" into "I can't find a job." So if you are serious about the prospect, you need to approach it as you would any other kind of business venture, with a plan and a presentation that tells everyone you are in it for the long haul.

CHAPTER TWELVE

Today's Retirement— A Time of Choices

"We are taught to anticipate aging as a process of shrinking. Surprisingly, it turns out to be in some respects a spreading out from the narrower focus of earlier life, a diffusing, a broadening, an opening of possibilities in a larger, more human world."

—JOHN S. MURPHY, FREDERIC M. HUDSON,
The Joy of Old

THE concept of retirement is changing. As people live longer, healthier lives, the idea that we will want to "retire," or as the thesaurus euphemistically puts it, "cease, come to an end, recede, retreat, expire, go away," or even "bow out," is no longer appropriate. We are more likely to think of retirement as a time when we are free from the obligation of working nine to five, and looking forward to lifestyle choices that include hobbies, travel, volunteer work, part-time employment—or even starting an entirely new career. At the peak of our professional lives, it's great to have time for rest and recreation—for a while—but then most people miss the challenge and excitement of a more demanding lifestyle.

Unfortunately, most enter these years without giving much thought to how they will spend their time. For them, retirement is a "going away from" rather than a "going to," and planning is limited to the money they will need to cover expenses. The quality of the life they'll soon be living is given little thought, and in far too many cases, life after the retirement party is short. The transition from an active to a passive life takes its toll, mentally, physically, emotionally, and socially. Vital, involved people go from being instigators and implementors of life to being observers. It doesn't have to be that way.

CASE STUDY: Jim B. is a tall, rangy, forty-two-year-old fireman. Proud of being in top physical condition, he works out daily, not just because his job demands it, but because he enjoys it. He is a finely tuned machine, mentally, emotionally, and physically alert; ready to spring into action at a moment's notice. He is good at what he does and confident that he can handle whatever comes his way. That is, he was until he reached retirement age.

Jim spent the first few months of retirement doing little more than hanging around the house, doing a little work on the yard and a little fishing. But he spent more time in front of the television than anywhere else. He even quit working out; it just didn't seem important anymore. He dropped into the firehouse two or three times a week, but really didn't feel like one of the gang anymore, so he soon stopped.

One morning Jim woke up and realized he didn't have any reason to get out of bed. The weight of a day-to-day existence without goals closed in around him. For Jim, that feeling was a wake-up call. At age forty-four, he returned to school to complete the degree he had started twenty-six years earlier. Three years later he graduated with a degree in social services, combining his academic knowledge with a lifetime of valuable experience to work with inner-city youth.

Jim is part of a whole cadre of retirees filling the classrooms of our colleges and universities. They bring real-world experience to academia and everyone benefits.

CASE STUDY: Bill M. was sixty-four. He has been in heavy manufacturing for over forty years, as an engineer, manufacturing manager, and plant manager. Highly regarded in the industry, he was known for his bulldog determination. It was hard for anyone, particularly Bill, to imagine him retiring. As he would say, "Work is my hobby." After his company went through a downsizing and his job was eliminated, he was determined to find a job as quickly as possible.

Bill believed he had several choices: consulting, going after venture capital to purchase a company, or looking for a job. What Bill did not consider were his wife's wishes. Sue and Bill had been married for forty-two years. They had five children and thirteen grandchildren. She has moved with him throughout his career, even when he was sent to Hong Kong. Whether or not Bill was ready for retirement, Sue wanted to spend more time together, and with their grandchildren.

It took a while to convince Bill that the two of them had the opportunity to create a whole new life, but in time he realized that if he became a consultant, they could combine their love of travel and time with the kids with his work.

Bill and Sue are not unusual. Couples who have had a clearly defined set of priorities based on the breadwinner's career often find a midlife career transition gives them the opportunity to make lifestyle choices together for the first time.

CASE STUDY: Harold L. came from a long line of attorneys. He fell into the profession, attending Harvard like his father, uncles, and grandfather before him, with little real thought of doing anything else. He served as a law clerk and then joined the family firm, gradually taking over more and more of the business as older relatives retired. The pattern was established. He assumed he would work until he was sixty and then retire himself. In the meantime, he went to work every day, made some reasonable investments that would ensure a comfortable retirement, and looked forward to golf with his friends at the club.

His wife, Jane, kept busy managing their social life and working on her own golf game. It was a traditional relationship and both considered themselves happy and well adjusted. Harold really didn't question whether or not he enjoyed his work; he had inherited his profession from his father and it was as much a part of who and what he was as the crooked smile he had inherited from his mother.

Harold turned sixty, left the firm, and he and Jane moved south to the land of year-round golf. Bright, physically fit, well-read people, the last thing they expected was for disillusionment to set in within the first year. As Harold said, "Golf just isn't much fun when it's all you have to look forward to day after day."

Neither of them had ever taken time to explore any hobbies other than golf. The other retirees they played with were equally out of contact with the "real" world. Their children were busy with their own lives, and moving to Florida meant they were too far away to enjoy their grandchildren. Two years later, Harold and Jane moved back north, rejoined their old church, and became active in the community. They had come home.

Harold and Jane made the mistake so many retirees make; they isolated themselves from the world they knew and the people they cared about most to enter a fantasy world of leisure.

CASE STUDY: Russ D. has just turned forty and fully expects to retire in two years, taking home a cool $6 million in stocks he earned as

VP of information services for a start-up telecommunications company he joined just three years before. He and his wife started their family late, so their children, Brenda and Charlie, will be three and a half and six when Dad comes home full-time.

Like most prospective retirees, Russ has spent absolutely no time or energy planning for retirement. He is heading for the finish line, and as he says, "I can stand on my head if I have to for two years." But is it the goal, or the challenge of reaching the goal, that is the most fun? It's unlikely that being a full-time dad and husband is going to be an easy transition for him, or his family, unless he has new goals and challenges to replace the ones he's leaving behind. Changing the environment is not going to change who he is: an achiever, a person who thrives on action.

The whole concept of retirement as "withdrawal from life" is an artificial one that has little meaning for today's midlife career transitioners. The Boomer generation is more attuned to activity than a sedentary life, so we must reevaluate our concept of retirement and think of it as a beginning—not an end. *I urge those who leave careers they have built over twenty or thirty or forty years to go into retirement with intent, with purpose, and with dreams. It is a time not to withdraw from life, but to choose life.*

Retirement is not an extended vacation, although most people imagine it will be like an unbroken chain of them. For these folks, the Golden Years are nothing more than fool's gold. Daily life continues. The lawn still needs mowing, meals need to be prepared, the same car gets flat tires and needs fixing. Your spouse irritates you in the same ways (except now you're together all the time!). There is no escape.

The biggest surprise for most new retirees is discovering their spouses are far from thrilled to have them around all the time. As one client said, "After a year my wife announced that either I had to get a job, or she would. We didn't need the money; she just couldn't take it anymore. I hadn't figured it out that *she* hadn't retired. I expected her to continue managing the household, helping with the grandchildren, doing volunteer work, and still find time to travel and do things with me. I didn't realize there just weren't that many hours in the day for her. I got a half-time job, and we're both happier."

Retirement doesn't just happen to one person. It happens to everyone in their lives: spouses, families, friends, even former coworkers. For spouses, too much togetherness can destroy an otherwise good relationship, unless both create new lives.

Retirement is a time of exploration, a time to identify the values that make life meaningful, to uncover those things that energize and excite you, that give you a sense of fulfillment and well-being. Sounds a lot like the process you use to determine a new career move, doesn't it? It should, because this is the stage of life you've been waiting for, and it deserves the best you have to offer. As Betty Friedan says in her book *The Fountain of Age*, "I am myself at this age. It took me all these years to put the missing pieces together, to confront my own age in terms of integrity and generativity, moving into the unknown future with comfort now, instead of being stuck in the past. I have never felt so free."

Thoughts About Retirement

Retirement shouldn't just happen. It should begin with looking back and thinking about what role work has played in your life. To create the next stage of your life, you must first understand why you made the choices you did in the past, then build upon those that excited you, and set aside those you disliked. Ask yourself these questions, or better yet, ask your partner to answer them with you. Then use them as a foundation for discussions that will shape your future.

1. How old were you when you got your first job? How much a part of your life has your work been?

2. How many of your friends and associates are affiliated with your work?

3. How much of your time and energies are spent in activities related to work? Create a detailed log of your typical week. Be sure to include the time you spend on peripheral activities such as preparing for work, shopping for business clothes, driving to and from work, business lunches and required social events, studying to remain current in your field, as well as the hours you spend on the job.

4. Describe the lifestyle you would choose if work were no longer a consideration. Where would you choose to live? How much has your career determined the choices you have made in your home, friends, car, club, social activities, restaurants, vacations, sports, and children's schools? How would you change them?

5. How much of your family's time and energies have been dominated by your work? Have you discussed with them what choices they wish they could have made? How would they like their lives to change now that you are retiring? Do you agree?

6. Will your spouse continue to work? How will this affect your retirement choices and lifestyle? Will you become the support system? How will you feel about that? Will you be able to travel, vacation, or take up new hobbies if your spouse is still working?

7. Will your retirement income make it possible for you to do the things you really enjoy?

8. How much of the conversation between you and your spouse is work-related? If you were to eliminate discussions of your children and work issues, what would you talk about?

9. List the ten things in your life that you are most proud of. How many of them are work-related? How closely are your self-esteem, self-confidence, and sense of self-worth related to your career?

10. What hobbies and interests have you developed over the years?

11. What have you always wanted to learn? What talents would you like to develop? What skills would you like to acquire?

Working by Choice

Retirement is all about choices, one of which is choosing whether or not to work. Work is a major part of life, and just because you've reached a particular age or stage of life doesn't mean it automatically loses importance. Memories are wonderful, but making them is generally more fun. Work is more than a paycheck; it's the sense of a job well done, the satisfaction that comes from knowing someone values what you do enough to pay for it, the good feeling that comes from being part of a group, and even the weariness that makes vacations and days off special. And then there's that identity thing. Whether or not we like to admit it, much of who and what we are is wrapped up in our work. The name of the company where we work subconsciously becomes a part of us, and when it's gone a little part of us goes too.

One retiree said, "I feel like a ship without a rudder." It is not surprising then, that many decide to return to work. Here are some of the reasons why:

- bored with enforced leisure

- want to be involved in the mainstream of life

- want to feel productive and accomplish something worthwhile

- enjoy the camaraderie of being part of a team

- want to bring some structure and order back to their lives

- want to feel needed and productive

- enjoy challenges

- think it will restore status, prestige

- believe working keeps them mentally, emotionally, and physically healthy

- like to work

- find weekends and vacations are more satisfying when they're working

- enjoy making money and the things it can buy

A psychologist friend who works with retirees tells me she often recommends that her patients go back to work, at least part-time. She says it "restores their dignity and brings back purpose to their lives."

People who choose to retire (or have the decision made for them) frequently believe they have no other options. Some retirees think they might like to work but say they don't try to find a job because:

- *"I've never looked for a job and don't know how. I don't even know how to write a résumé."*

- *"I guess I'm afraid of rejection or even of being laughed at; it's easier to let friends think I don't want to work than to take a chance."*

- *"For so long I've talked about looking forward to retirement, I hate to admit now that I'm not enjoying it."*

- *"Companies want young people. They won't hire anyone over age fifty."*

- *"I'd have to go back to school, or at least take some computer classes."*

- *"I've earned my retirement and I shouldn't have to work."*

- *"I just can't decide what I want to do, or even if I want to work."*

Your age and where you stand career-wise influence your retirement choices. A forty-year-old in a high-risk, high-action job may be waiting for his stock options to set him free in a year or two. He's looking forward to high living in retirement. The fifty-six-year-old, forced out in a corporate downsizing in order to make room for younger workers, is likely to be concerned about facing age discrimination in finding a job. The sixty-eight-year-old who has been retired for several years is generally well aware of the myth of retirement bliss and would give it all up in a minute to be back on the job.

As one client remarked, "There are as many stages to the third third of life as there are to the first. Sometimes I think it's like going through childhood all over again, only this time everyone expects me to know what I'm doing. How can I? I haven't been fifty before; it's uncharted territory." The key is planning that allows the flexibility to grow and change as you move through your own "stages," understanding that from midlife on it's more important than ever to think of your life in three-to-five-year segments, because what is enjoyable and fulfilling today may be quite different a few years from now. The biggest mistake retirees make is to imagine that the choices they make on retirement day are for always. They create their own prisons and sentence themselves to life sentences without parole without even knowing it.

Working is not an "either-or" proposition. Today, temporary, part-time, consulting, and contract workers are a significant part of the workforce. You can start a small home business, join an electronic network of entrepreneurs; there are more ways than ever before of "getting work that needs doing, done." Some say "jobs" are an anachronism. However, as Alex Comfort says in his book *A Good Age,* "What the retired need . . . isn't leisure, it's occupation. Two weeks is about the ideal length of time to retire."

Dealing with Age Discrimination

So, what if you decide to go back to work? It is naive to assume age discrimination does not exist. Whether it is the dragon waiting to rise up and devour you or merely a slight bump in the road depends upon the industry, the company, the hiring manager, and, quite frankly, how much they need your background and skills. The biggest obstacle in the age-discrimination war, however, may be your attitude. If you believe your age is an advantage, it probably will be; if you believe your age is a disadvantage, it definitely will be. Having said that, however, there are ways you can overcome or at least deal with age discrimination when it does exist. First, never assume you are being discriminated against because of your age. Check out these possibilities first.

- *Match of skills and experience with the job requirements:* Example: not having a CPA or SEC experience is going to screen someone out of top finance positions in many companies, regardless of all other experience.

- *Cultural match:* If you are a methodical person, professionally attired in a dark suit, white shirt, and tie when you interview at a high-tech firm, you might as well carry a sign saying NO MATCH HERE! And let's face it, if everyone there is under thirty-five, it may mean neither you nor they would be comfortable.

- *Incomplete résumé:* Are you leaving out significant portions of your professional experience? If your résumé doesn't tell the complete story, you are selling yourself short and they have no way of knowing what you can really do.

- *Interview presentation:* This is a sales presentation. Would you honestly buy this product? How convincing are you? Do you know your story? What can you do for the company? Don't just assume as one client said, "They should know what I can do."

- *Technical competence:* If you are not completely comfortable handling all your own clerical duties, everything else takes second place. Companies are not going to hire a secretary to take care of you.

- *Flexibility and compatibility with manager:* The reality is you may well be working for someone who is significantly younger than you are. Is your own "age discrimination" showing?

- *Management style:* Older managers are used to a clear delineation of authority and expect direction or even "permission" before proceeding. Their younger counterparts rely on the adage "It's better to ask forgiveness than permission." This can cause confusion or even the perception that the older person lacks confidence or enthusiasm for the task.

- *Physical fitness:* There is certainly less tolerance for lack of physical fitness in older applicants than in younger ones. Whether or not this is fair, there is a certain logic to it. The fifty-year-old who is sixty pounds overweight and obviously out of condition is more likely to have a heart attack than a thirty-five-year-old in the same condition. You have control over this variable. Start exercising. You will feel better in the interview and everywhere else.

- *Salary requirements:* A fifty-year-old averages 40 percent higher salary requirements than someone ten years younger. You'll have to prove to a potential employer that it is economically a wise decision to hire you. You may have financial flexibility and believe an interesting job is more important than the money, but the person who is interviewing you won't know unless you tell them.

Second, recognize when it really is age discrimination. If a company:

- eliminates a position to get rid of an older worker,

- doesn't consider anyone over forty,

- makes it unpleasant for the older person by giving them menial tasks or "shelving" them in semiretirement roles,

- allows "age harassment," including crude banter in the workplace that pokes fun of older people or suggests they should retire to make room for younger workers,

- sets arbitrary age limits on employment,

- has a policy not to provide training for anyone over fifty "because older people can't learn new technology . . . are too inflexible to learn . . . or will be retiring soon, so it's a waste of money,"

- tells applicants they are "overqualified" and won't be content in the position . . .

. . . it's age discrimination and should not be tolerated.

One manager constantly urged his sixty-two-year-old employee to "Take more time off. At your age you should be relaxing and spending more time watching sunsets with your wife." While the manager had good intentions, he was presuming to impose his own preferences on someone who happened to be enjoying work immensely and had no intention of slowing up. This kind of subtle discrimination, spoken in kindness, can be the most harmful of all. It is difficult to respond to and can eventually make the employee so uncomfortable he leaves the company. Regardless of intent, discrimination is wrong.

The Age Discrimination in Employment Act (ADEA) of 1967 made it illegal to deny employment because of age and eliminated mandatory retirement in government and private sectors. Age discrimination in hiring, discharge, pay, promotions, fringe benefits, and other aspects of employment is also illegal. The ADEA applies to private employers of twenty or more workers as well as to government offices and employment agencies. Various exceptions apply, so anyone considering legal action should research the laws. Midlife career transitioners who think they're too young to be affected by age discrimination take note: the laws apply to anyone age forty and over.

Major discrimination lawsuits and large settlements have heightened awareness of the law. This can be good news and bad news for the older applicant. Rather than take a chance, some employers disregard applications from older people, thus denying the applicant equal opportunity to compete for the position. It is certainly possible to win a court case if, indeed, the evidence shows discrimination; however, carefully consider whether the result will be worth the money, time, and energy it will take to pursue legal action. If the end result is that you're offered a job, do you really want it? Monetary awards may be satisfying, but if the struggle decreases your life span, it may not be worth it. One of the major disadvantages to legal action is that it distracts you from getting on with your life, including the search for a great job in a company that will value you and your experience. Think of it this way: the company that discriminates because of age or anything else is the loser in the end.

There are very strict rules governing time frames for making charges and filing a claim. If you're considering a claim, keep detailed written records, whenever possible. Include dates, names and testimony of witnesses, a description of your job and work history with the company, copies of termination notices, and specific examples of when you were treated differently than other employees. For further information, contact: U.S. Equal Employment Opportunity Commission (EEOC); toll-free: 1-800-USA-EEOC.

Volunteering: the Gifts of Time and Talents

Wearing hard hats and blue jeans, with tools hanging from their belts, former President Jimmy and First Lady Rosalynn Carter have traveled the world, taking volunteerism to new heights as they work alongside people from all walks of life to provide homes for those who could not otherwise afford them. Nothing has done as much to restore respect for Americans throughout the rest of the world as these caring people who are willing to put their time and talents to work making the world a better place.

The Carters have transformed the image of volunteerism from elderly ladies with big flowered hats and white gloves having charity teas to one of men and women working together to lift beams and carry buckets of sand. Calluses have replaced framed certificates, and friendships have replaced paternalism. President Carter has used his experience and expertise to negotiate peace between warring nations, and to help countries achieve their first-ever free elections. His face is probably recognized more throughout the world today than it was when he was in the Oval Office. Studies show anywhere from 60 to 76 percent of people over the age of fifty-five are involved in volunteer activities. According to ICR Research Group, 15.5 million people over age sixty contribute 3.6 billion hours a year of service.

Why do people choose to volunteer during their retirement years? It offers them a chance to :

1. Support a cause or mission they believe in

2. Meet people with like interests

3. Be productive, needed, use their skills and talents

4. Learn

5. Enjoy travel that lets them meet local people and get to know the area on a more personal level

6. Reap emotional/spiritual rewards

7. Get involved in current events

8. Attain positions of honor and recognition

9. Start another career

10. Develop networking contacts

There is no training ground for retirement. Each of us enters this uncharted territory and becomes a settler in a myriad of ways. Whether you choose a new career, volunteerism, travel, education, or hobbies and recreation, you'll have a new awareness of the world, and a better understanding that it is the journey, not the destination, that really counts.

How Likely Are You to Enjoy Retirement?

Although it is a relatively new concept historically, the myth of retirement is so firmly entrenched in our culture that it's almost sacrilegious to question its validity or desirability. Many feel they've earned it and they're going to take what they're entitled to . . . regardless of whether or not they're ready to leave a successful career. To contemplate the wholesale retirement of the seventy-six million Baby Boomers born between 1946 and 1964 is to imagine one of the greatest social shifts our world has ever experienced. Fortunately, for both the economy and the stability of our society, few of these independent thinkers are likely to buy the entitlement rationale or forgo the power they wield by settling for a rocking chair and the front stoop. They've thrown away the clock and aren't particularly interested in whether they are approaching or bypassing the mid-century mark. They're too busy to care. Part of the reason is that the goalpost has been moved. Baby Boomers are likely to live two or three decades longer than previous generations and they have every intention of enjoying those decades.

It's impossible to predict whether or not someone will enjoy the retirement experience, but positive responses to these questions are good indicators that you will.

- Are you generally a person who enjoys life? Do you consider yourself to be adaptable and flexible?

- Do you have good relationships with close family and friends? Are your children and parents well established and unlikely to require large amounts of your time, money, or energies?

- Do you have a strong sense of values and mission in life? Do you have a strong self-image?

- Are you optimistic about retirement? Do you have fond memories of your parents' retirement years? Do you have a positive perception of aging?

- Do you have well-developed interests and hobbies outside of work?

- Are you in good health?

- Are you secure financially?

In general, the more balanced a person's life before retirement, the more likely that the transition will go well. Some people use work to escape from problems, but in retirement there are very few places to hide. Sharing goals and interests, looking forward rather than backward, and finding productive ways to spend your days and use your talents make each day something to look forward to. There is much to think about in the words of the philosopher Søren Kierkegaard, "Philosophy is perfectly right in saying that life must be understood backward. But then one forgets the other clause— that it must be lived forward."

CHAPTER THIRTEEN

Career Entrepreneur

"The fact that your awareness of mortality shows up at midlife is wonderful, because it pushes you as nothing else will into respecting your own happiness, and your happiness will unerringly draw you to your genius."

—BARBARA SHER, *It's Only Too Late If You Don't Start Now*

THE concept of career entrepreneurship is that each of us is responsible for our own careers. Midlife career transition is the time to become an entrepreneur, to "own" your career, creating it with vision and imagination and managing it by using your talents and skills to their greatest advantage. That might mean taking on a new role at your current place of work, becoming a consultant or project manager for hire. Whether this is frightening or exciting depends upon your nature, attitude, and how well you handle the responsibility.

Careers in the future are more likely to be cyclical than linear. Those entering the workforce today will be likely to change careers several times and, no doubt, continue working well into their later years. Career cycles mesh well with the complexities of modern life, where change has made it impossible to predict anything very far in advance. While that vision of the future may be unsettling to some, cycling through different careers is something the career entrepreneur takes in stride. She doesn't see the end of a working relationship with a particular company as a cataclysmic event, but rather as part of a natural progression toward another interesting opportunity.

A key factor in career entrepreneurship is recognizing when it's time to move on. In a career cycle, the start of a new job is the most intense period, when you are the most productive. Your energies and enthusiasm will be the greatest and your commitment the strongest. It is the courtship stage, when all things seem not only possible, but probable.

Most people eventually plateau, however, and reach a stage when the work is just not as interesting as it once was. You've been there, done that, and the spark is gone. Quite simply, this plateau usually means you've stopped learning. Sometimes you can sidestep a plateau for a time by taking on more responsibilities, including mentoring others or taking advantage of educational or professional development opportunities. At some point, however, you find you're just hanging on. You've lost your enthusiasm, your energy decreases, and you have a nagging feeling that it is time to move on. Often referred to as "burnout," it's really incredible boredom. It is human nature to stick with the familiar, but you just aren't having much fun anymore and you begin to feel trapped and helpless. Career entrepreneurs are visionaries constantly looking for new opportunities. They take risks (and may occasionally go in the wrong direction), but their flexibility, adaptability, and unfailing confidence make it possible for them to create strategies to find new directions. It takes courage and initiative to start a new career cycle; first you need to recognize that you have the power to make the change. People usually go through four stages before they make the break:

- denial that the old job is no longer satisfying
- recognition that a change might be a good idea
- willingness to explore possibilities
- readiness to take action

Career entrepreneurship is about doing *what* you must, *because* you must, *when* you must.

Any good entrepreneur can benefit from an advisory board, and managing your career is no exception. Establish a corporate board of directors and, just as you would for any other corporation, choose people with the specific expertise you need. Include dreamers and efficiency experts, design engineers, salespeople and marketers, financial analysts, and public-relations and technology gurus. Think carefully before you include close friends or relatives, whose biases and personal agendas may prevent them from being effective board members. You need the kind of objectivity that you won't get from people who know you too well. Create a mission statement that provides focus and direction and bear in mind that your life, and the career that supports and enriches it, is an ongoing process. If you are going to renew, you must *anticipate,* and your board can help you recognize when it is time to change. The role of your board will be to help you brainstorm ideas, discuss philosophy, analyze procedures, and provide the fifty-thousand-foot view as well as practical down-to-earth strategies and tactics. Most of all, their job is to encourage you, to be the "wind in your sails."

Viewing a career as a series of cycles prepares you for its ups and downs and keeps you alert. It's okay to take chances, to experiment. Remember that we rarely learn as much from success as we do from failure. Trust your instincts, avoid analysis paralysis, and recognize that the answers are within you.

Forget Corporate Ladders; Go Where the Jobs Are

Are you ready to adopt the attitude of a career entrepreneur? If you've been with a company for many years and have successfully climbed a career ladder, you may have difficulty understanding the "ladderless" organization, but—ladders or no ladders—companies do not hire someone over age fifty with the expectation of "developing" them. Promotions may come, but they're rare. As the manager of your own career, chances are you'll have to move to another company to get that raise and title. One of the most frequent comments I hear from midlife clients is, "I want to find a stable company where I can stay until I retire." This, my friends, does not exist. Accepting that reality is the first step to assuming control of your own career progression.

A New Role in Your Current Company

My advice to people at midlife when they're itching for a change is to move into the role of elder statesman or stateswoman and look for opportunities to function as an internal consultant at their current place of work.

CASE STUDY: Joan S. was head of the information-services department of a local utility that served a major metropolitan area. She had been with the organization for eighteen years and was well liked and respected. An attractive woman in her late forties, she was consistently professional in both appearance and performance. She was also bored to death.

She said, "I feel like I'm living my life over and over, like a bad play that just won't end. I'd give anything to do something new and interesting." She assured me that she had no real desire to leave the organization; she liked the people and the culture and felt they were doing good work in the community (of course, eligibility for a retirement pension in a few years was no small consideration!). Information services was an area she knew well, but she felt the management work she was doing no longer held any real challenge. Her technical staff seemed to have all the fun, while she handled people issues and administrative tasks.

The answer for Joan wasn't all that difficult to find. I convinced her to negotiate a position as the IS internal consultant for the company, and to start turning over day-to-day responsibilities of the department to members of her staff. She would be providing opportunities for their career development while adding new dimensions to her own role. Her boss saw the advantages and agreed to the change. In her new role, she continued to have final oversight in the information-services area, but in the meantime, her time and "wisdom" were better spent serving as a resource throughout the organization.

Approaching the job search in your old familiar office with a consultant's perspective plays well to a midlife career transitioner's strengths. You may identify a consulting role within the company, as Joan did, or look for one in the outside world; but whichever you choose, you have the credibility and the background to inspire confidence and make a success of the position.

New Challenges in a Small Company

A basic rule of marketing is to "fish where the fish are." In other words, find the customer who has a need for your product. It might be hard to find your way there, but you won't come home with an empty creel. Go with a small company—where the fish are. Large companies are cumbersome, slow moving, and multifaceted, like big, awkward ships plowing ponderously through the water. Small companies are like sleek jet boats, turning on a dime to quickly solve customer problems, moving resources on a moment's notice, and changing direction to take advantage of the prevailing wind. Decision making is quick and decisive. Staff is limited, so everyone wears several hats, making decisions on the spot that can affect the entire future of the company. Your experience will be invaluable to such a company.

Pulling Teams Together; Consulting

Pulling disparate cultures together into a smoothly functioning workforce in the wake of a merger is an enormous challenge. Not the least of the problem is the fact that employees are often scattered worldwide. Whole departments at the local level are eliminated, their responsibilities taken over by a central office known only through impersonal e-mail messages, with new procedures, policies, and software systems. The various entities have very little connection with corporate headquarters and resentment builds on both sides. In these cases, older workers with extensive background in the field can be very effective in building the trust that is necessary to mediate differences and create an efficient organization.

People tend to trust someone who is older. This can be a major asset in finding opportunities with consulting firms. Consulting is an extremely competitive business, where faith and trust are the most important commodities. Having "elder statesmen and stateswomen" on a consulting staff is an enormous advantage, particularly in the initial stages of contract proposals when the company needs someone who can quickly analyze the prospective client's needs, develop the response to the RFP (request for proposal), and make the formal presentation of the company's qualifications.

Working Overseas: Short Term, High Pay

Multinational companies frequently have difficulty finding managers who are willing to work overseas for short-term projects because people are reluctant to uproot families or be away from their homes for extended periods. An added concern is finding someone who is sensitive to cultural differences and experienced with international deals. At midlife, you may be very willing (even eager?) to take on international assignments, looking forward to bringing your spouse along and taking advantage of the opportunity to travel on your own after the assignment. The company will breathe easy knowing they have an experienced manager at the helm. Manufacturing companies are prime beneficiaries of this resource, as they open and close plants worldwide to take advantage of optimum labor and material sources. If you are a retired plant manager, you are a highly desirable commodity in this job market.

Short-term assignments abound in the new marketplace, where rapid change and the high speed of communication have made it impossible for companies to guarantee long-term employment. In hiring you, they are getting a highly qualified employee who will require only minimum orientation before being fully productive. Executive temping is another option you might want to check out. These are senior managers who are hired to take over for executives who are ill, working on special projects, or taking sabbaticals. They are often hired when a company is going through a merger or acquisition, relocating, restructuring, expanding internationally, going public, or even trying to turn itself around in the face of imminent financial disaster. A number of high-profile executives known as "turnaround artists" command incredibly high salaries, complete with multimillion-dollar bonuses and stock options, and a waiting list of companies seeking their services. As soon as they get a company back on its feet, they move on to another challenge. They are having too much fun to consider retiring and making too much money to consider full-time employment.

Service Industries

What is the fastest-growing consumer market in the country? Whether you're in a coffee shop or a time-share office, a life-insurance agency or a golf club, the person behind the counter is more and more likely to be over fifty. As Boomers move toward retirement, they bring huge buying power. If you are interested in sales, there is great opportunity for jobs, full- or part-time, selling them products and services in hospitality, travel, investments, health care, luxury and efficiency living, insurance, and take-out gourmet foods. All are competing for Baby Boomers' dollars, and who better to sell the products than their peers?

Mobile telephones, e-mail, the virtual workplace—a work community where people are always "on the run" and rarely meet face-to-face is invariably going to experience huge gaps in communication. You have a lifetime dealing with people and can be the catalyst to bring people together. This is another great selling point for you when you are marketing your services to potential employers

Companies are specifically targeting older workers in their hiring for a number of reasons, including work ethics, flexible hours, people skills, productivity, likelihood they will stay with the job, sense of responsibility, customer-service orientation, higher level of basic skills (i.e., reading, writing, and mathematics), and lower absenteeism. Studies such as those conducted by the Commonwealth Fund and AARP publicize the age advantage, and with the increased need for contingent labor, possibilities are bound to expand. You have more opportunities to continue or begin a career than ever before, at the same time the workplace desperately needs your maturity, experience, and skills. As Ken Dychtwald says in his book *Age Wave,* "We are witnessing the end of yesterday's retirement, with Grandpa asleep on the porch, the gold watch the company gave him ticking in his vest pocket, and his friends coming over later to go fishing or play cards or checkers. This picture is giving way to a more involved mixture of work and leisure that will soon become standard."

Know the Marketplace

In order to market a product, you have to know the product well, its strengths and its potential, but it's equally important to know the marketplace. The old world of work that evolved out of the industrial age is changing rapidly, and it isn't just the fact that the corporate ladder is gone, or that lifetime employment with one company is a thing of the past. It's also how work is done within the organization. Before you can become a career entrepreneur and effectively market yourself as a job candidate, business owner, or consultant, you have to understand the changes that are taking place.

Companies are becoming mini-centers of commerce, little cities contracting for services, facilitating business between customer, vendor, and producer, providing the communication link, managing the process, and handling the details that make it all work, outsourcing the majority of their work to smaller companies and to people like you, who are entrepreneurs of your own independent businesses, your careers.

More and more companies are restructuring their organizations so their leaders can focus on running the operation, providing the vision and the direction, setting the course, and bringing in resources only as they need them. This includes everything from accounting to customer service to design engineering, from personnel management to information services and even packaging and delivery. Dell Computer uses over eighty thousand people to do its work, only fifteen thousand of whom are full-time employees. EDS (Ross Perot's old company), and its host of consultant-company followers, have made whole businesses of managing the information-service needs of other companies. Toyota outsources the production of over 75 percent of its component parts, and the Ford Motor Company supports numerous small manufacturers whose only customer is Ford. These are just the tip of the iceberg. The opportunities for someone with an entrepreneurial spirit are nearly unlimited.

You will be as likely to work out of your home in the future as out of a company-provided office space. As a telecommuter, you may work directly with corporate customers, spending little or no time with your employer other than to send in your expense form by e-mail and receive your check through automatic deposit. You will respond to requests to provide services, handle projects that vary from days to even years, and step in to provide help during crunch times. You will be working for yourself and focusing on your own career success.

People: the Competitive Advantage

Jack F. Welch, Jr., CEO of General Electric, once said, "The consuming passion of each of our companies must be to become so fast and so lean and so close to the customer that the value nub is always in our sights. We now know where productivity—real and limitless productivity—comes from . . . It comes from engaging every single mind in the organization." Technology is increasing the potential to develop new products at an exponential rate and making it possible for people around the world to learn about them in minutes. In today's fast-paced world, leadership at the top is no longer enough. Leadership must come from every person in the organization and everyone must be a career entrepreneur, self-directed and willing to make decisions on the spot, without waiting for direction. The companies that can recruit the best people will have the competitive edge.

Career entrepreneurs care about what they are doing, know why they are doing it, and believe their work has meaning beyond earning a paycheck. One CEO of a major high-tech company told me, "It's not what we *know* our employees will have to know tomorrow that we're worried about, but what they will *need* to know tomorrow, that we have no idea of today, that will make the difference in our company's survival." He said, "Don't send us anyone who is looking for security, for stability, where we can tell them exactly what we'll need them to do today, tomorrow, and next year. We need people who can handle ambiguity and change, because the only thing we can really guarantee is that there will be constant change."

Goals: Blinders or Roadways?

People, like companies, must have more than goals. They must have a vision of where they are going that encompasses the way they function, the essence of who they are, the way they feel about themselves as individuals, and how they relate to others. If we know who and what we are, we can deal with anything that happens. If we know only what our goals and objectives are, anything new that does not match our expectations throws us into confusion and chaos. Our core values must provide the map for how we evaluate situations and opportunities.

Goals can create tunnel vision. It sounds like heresy to suggest any person or any organization should attempt to function without goals, but perhaps we need to rethink how useful goals are in a world that is moving and changing at warp speed. You can't afford to wear blinders. You must constantly reevaluate, reconsider, and reconnoiter. As a career entrepreneur, you will need goals to keep you on a viable career track; the trick is to keep challenging your perceptions, to ask fundamentally new questions throughout the process, to test the validity of your assumptions and make adjustments.

One of your greatest challenges when you begin full-time or contract work with a new organization will be to quickly identify the characteristics of a company and, like a chameleon, blend into the background and become a part of them. Companies are living, ever-evolving organisms that have the capacity to renew themselves through good or bad choices. They have a language of their own and a set of values understood by the people within them. They have their own ways of doing things and making decisions. Like any living organism, they are never static.

Adjusting to Change

Survival depends upon learning to adjust, almost instinctively, to change. Remember the lesson of the dinosaur, who was too cumbersome, too inflexible to survive, and don't let it happen to you. Replace a need for certainty with the firm belief that you have the power to evolve—whatever the future holds. Have faith in your ability to build a bridge from the past to the future. The message is, it is okay for you to risk, to question, to think outside of the box.

The workplace is shifting from one of obedience and domination to cooperation, mutual respect, and shared responsibility. It is filled with networks of relationships, of integrated systems of people and small companies working together. In a rapidly changing world, it's not enough to learn a skill; we need to learn how to learn. We must have a systems perspective rather than a task perspective, to ask ourselves, "How does what I am doing fit into the big picture?" The workplace of the future will be based on interdependence, the ideal environment for career entrepreneurs.

Process Flow

Process flow is replacing the little kingdoms of functional departments and isolated silos, creating fluid roles and responsibilities and forcing employees to respond quickly and efficiently. Jack Welch speaks of the "boundaryless" behavior that is needed to be successful today. "Boundaryless behavior laughs at the concept of little kingdoms called engineering, manufacturing, and marketing sending each other specs and memos, and instead gets them all together in a room to wrestle with issues as a team."

In this system, the process "owner" coordinates the total operation of a specific function throughout the organization, like an invisible thread that goes through every department, ensuring continuous communication, availability of resources, and time lines. This owner ties everyone together to create a seamless "flow." One company with distribution centers and manufacturing plants worldwide uses process flow for all major support areas, i.e., human resources, information services, purchasing, distribution, and accounting. Their employees have several supervisors, including the local plant manager, the head of their support-service function (i.e., director of finance), and a process owner (i.e., accounts payable). They work in multiple areas and projects at the same time, so they must be very flexible, work both independently and as part of a team, and be willing to take responsibility for problem solving. In a process-flow system, you may "own" one process and be involved in several others, and although your time will primarily be spent using your specific expertise, you will be more of an internal consultant rather than working on predictable tasks listed in a job description. Midlife career transitioners find this process-ownership role very comfortable.

Project Management

More and more companies are hiring full-time project managers to handle specific projects as interim assignments or contract work. These projects have defined outcomes and require bringing resources of people and materials together under cross-functional teams of subject-area experts for a limited period. It is entirely possible to work on more than one project at a time. Project management is an ideal role for midlife career transitioners, particularly if you are willing to get formal credentials, including university courses and certification.

Permanent, full-time employees will be outnumbered in the future by visitors, outsiders without ties to the company's goals or to each other. This can result in major communication problems, somewhat like bringing the United Nations together without interpreters. Project management provides the common language and methodology to make it all work. Acquiring certification as a project manager professional (PMP) can create career mobility that bypasses the constraints of functions or even industries and expands the possibilities for marketing yourself.

Information the Tool, Communication the Challenge

Everyone's talking, but is anybody listening? E-mail and voice-mail messages travel in an uninterrupted flow, but there is little real assurance anyone is listening on the other end. With more communication channels than ever before, the big question is how much communication is going on.

"Lifelong learning" is more than a pleasant cliché as we enter the new millennium. It's real. Companies and employees both are facing the fact that they must continually learn or become obsolete in the marketplace. Information technology is driving the world, and people who can manage it will manage the world. People who are content to ride along in the backseat will soon find themselves sitting by the roadside. Which are you?

Currently, employees with backgrounds in information services are the most in demand. In the future, companies will assume that everyone has a background in information services. No one today would think of assuring their employer that they have a background in using electricity. Of course they do. How would they function in their daily life if they didn't use electricity? However, as technology replaces workers, and increased efficiencies brought about by mergers and acquisitions eliminate whole departments, companies are going to be able to pick and choose the most qualified employees, and the "haves" and "have nots" of tomorrow's marketplace will be directly dependent upon knowledge acquisition and usage. Learning must be lifelong, because the technological revolution has just begun and it will be impossible to function at any stage of life without being part of it.

As the workplace loses the continuity of people working together over a large number of years, personal and professional relationships are becoming more separate, and this is a concern for our sense of community, of belonging to a larger whole. Working on a contract with someone you never expect to meet again changes the dynamics and creates a professional anonymity in which personal values and ethics can be separated from the pragmatics of a momentary professional goal.

It is logical to assume that not everyone will either wish to become a career entrepreneur or have the skills, self-confidence, and determination to do so. Companies composed of a multitude of independent operators rather than a stable, permanent workforce are going to find their greatest challenge is continuity, keeping everyone on track until the job is done. Individual stress is likely to be higher and corporate stress will be through the ceiling unless there is a good match between individual and group values and goals, and both formal and informal processes for ongoing and honest communication are encouraged. As a career entrepreneur, it will be critical that you carefully select the companies where you work.

The real challenge will be to reinvent a sense of community, for people are inherently integral to each other and it isn't enough to *know* someone by e-mail. In the virtual workplace, we will need to create mini-communities to provide the relationships once developed over long careers with the same company. In our professional lives, we can do this by networking with people we work with on projects, through professional associations, by forming informal alliances with people and small companies who can provide related services on contracts together, and through volunteer organizations.

The Paradigm Shift

The paradigm has changed and we must change with it. Very soon, the *place* we work will no longer have definition.

The age of technology has redefined work and separated it from a place, creating the virtual workplace, a nebulous entity with invisible, intangible connections between people and projects. It is possible for people to "work together" without ever seeing each other, to accomplish goals and celebrate achievements without sharing a smile or a slap on the back, to be integral parts of multimillion-dollar projects without having a clue as to who the other players are or what they are doing. It is a world both complex and vague, a fantasy world of the imagination.

The old world was simple. There were rules, which most of us knew and which most of us followed, most of the time. When we didn't, there were usually consequences. It was a world based on *certainty*, on predictability, on control, on layers of responsibility, on rules that told us who we were and that defined our relationship to others.

The new world of work is complex. Some will be more comfortable with the old ways, some more comfortable with the new. People who are more intuitive, more independent, and more fascinated by the future than the past will thrive on the new style; others, more conservative by nature and more comfortable in a world where rules and relationships were clear, will need to find full-time jobs at the core of organizations. The basic premise of being career entrepreneurs is that all of us will need to direct our own lives and make the choices for ourselves.

The Bottom Line Is Attitude

In the past, work was synonymous with "labor," implying "burden," "drudgery," and joyless plodding. I believe the world of work is changing for the better.

Lifelong employment with one company is gone, loyalty to one company a thing of the past. The people where you work are not your family. Good riddance to that idea! Underneath the concern (and panic), there is a new energy in the workplace and a commitment to mutual success that didn't exist when people turned their careers (and lives, to a large part) over to the person who paid their salary.

In the old corporate world, people were cogs in the industrial wheel; in the new world of work, they are valued as intellectual resources and recognized as partners. Employer and employee enter into mutually beneficial relationships and leave them when they are no longer useful. Harsh as this might sound, it also opens up whole new opportunities for setting and meeting personal goals.

Nowhere is this dramatic change more keenly felt than by people in midlife transition. It can be a culture shock and a time of awakening. As for a butterfly leaving the cocoon, it can be frightening or incredibly energizing to realize you and only you are responsible for creating your life's work, for making choices on how and where you will invest your energies, and then know the thrill of achieving the goals you choose.

Quit today and rehire yourself tomorrow! Become CEO of your own career! You are captain of this ship! You are a free agent, playing your best for the team, but moving to a new team when the time is right. You are an entrepreneur, constantly renewing your marketability to meet the needs of your customers. You are an explorer, challenged and excited about the frontier of your own life.

Midlife career transition is a time of knowing and being. The answers for each of us are inside us, but with knowing also comes the responsibility to take action—action that may require lifestyle changes. "Being" is wholeness that comes when your energies are focused on things you genuinely care about, without regard for external rewards. It is the state in which you celebrate your natural talents and your energies seem limitless. Like birds who fly and fish who swim, it's your natural habitat.

Knowledge + Experience = Wisdom

Wisdom cannot be implanted, transplanted, or given as a gift. It must be earned. The main job of the elders of a society is to inspire others to believe in the potential of the future, to assume leadership, to move beyond themselves to a wider and clearer vision of what can be.

Data is easily acquired and discarded. It does not require a great deal of intelligence to gather and has no value in and of itself. Information is a step up. It's data plus context, combined in a useful manner. Knowledge is the practical application of information to new situations. Wisdom goes beyond the known to help us make considered judgments and form worthwhile opinions on things that cannot be proven by the past or easily projected into the future. It cannot be acquired without extensive life experience because it moves into the realm of subjectivity where judgment, instinct, and intuition blur.

Longitudinal studies by scientists, including Gisela Labouvie-Vief, K. Werner Schaie, and James Birren, debunk the idea that intellectual capabilities diminish with age. We probably "think" *differently* as we grow older and very well may use different criteria for making decisions, but there is solid evidence that intellectual capabilities actually increase with age. Wisdom is the practical application of knowledge in enough life situations that we can generally accept the validity of our instincts in order to reach sound conclusions that cannot be objectively "proven." In midlife, we are ready to bring wisdom to our lives, to our work, and to our society.

It is the natural role of the elders of a society to remind us that values, beliefs, priorities, and insights into human relationships are the highest priorities, that the "why" is much more important than the "how," and that choices based on the long-term evolution of the human spirit should take precedence over momentary achievement. It is the time to be the most creative of all. It is the time to be a career entrepreneur, the most empowering experience of all.

Index

Page numbers in italic denote illustrations; those in bold denote charts.